The Vanishing Veil

Marge Cuddeback

ISBN 0-9711308-0-9
Published By
Empowering Light
815 Mohican Way
Emerald Hills, CA 94062

Death is a beginning not an end. It is simply a transition to another dimension that has a higher rate of frequency. It is a giant step in our ongoing process of evolution.

We are all capable of higher things than what we have previously applied our mental abilities to. Realize this, go beyond your rational mind and enter the dimension of spirituality.

"We're not a physical person having a spiritual experience, but we're a spiritual being having a human experience."
— Barbara Marciniak in *Bringers of the Dawn*

Acknowledgments

I am deeply grateful to all of those who have consented to have their reading, regression, and/or clearing discussed in this book. To protect my clients' privacy, their true identity is not revealed. My heartfelt gratitude goes out to all of them.

My special thanks and love to my children, Laura Gordon, my oldest daughter, my son-in-law Brad Gordon, my middle daughter, Barbara Shea, and my youngest daughter, Erin Shea, for their continued love, support, encouragement and faith in this project and in me.

Thanks also to my two granddaughters, Lisa Gordon and Brianna Shea, for bringing a sweetness to my life that soars way beyond words.

I am also grateful for the transcribing assistance of Sue Hamilton and Karen McGee, and Karen's belief in this book and her years of endearing encouragement.

My gratitude to Mike Sibitz, a friend from my college years, for suggesting the title of this book.

I also want to thank Tony Stubbs, author of *An Ascension Handbook* for his insightful input.

My great appreciation to Marisa Maldonado for her time and computer expertise. And Anne Knudsen for the photography.

Thanks also to Linda Baker and Jillian Auberger who took time out of their busy schedules to help bring this book to completion.

I am grateful to every client who has attended my seminars, or who has had a reading, regression and/or clearing with me over the years. Thanks also to all my clients' "spirit friends and family" who came through me to help to heal the loss many of them were feeling over the death of their loved one.

Contents

Dedication

This book is dedicated to the departed loved ones in my immediate family, most of whom I lost during a 13-year period. I have listed them in the order that I lost them.

Mick Graham, oldest brother
Stephen Michael Shea, son
Fred Graham, father
Jerry Shea, husband
Pat Markham, sister

Introduction

The following are true-life cases I've encountered while acting as a metaphysical/psychic counselor for the past 25 years. I have included my own personal history so that you, the reader, might come to have a better understanding of the forces which have shaped my life and have subsequently led to the writing of this book. For many years now I have felt a very strong pull to write this book and get these stories and this information out into the public eye. Know that if you find yourself reading these words, it is not by accident or happenstance. (There *are* no coincidences in this universe!)

This book is a quick glimpse into a world which is just now beginning to reveal itself to those who are searching, and with this in mind, it will probably raise more questions for you than it will answer. Know that this is as it should be.

It is my hope that one or more of these true stories will touch you, inspire your own healing; will help you open, shift, and ultimately see a little more clearly through the veil that separates us from the other side. The Vanishing Veil.

Vanishing Veil

My Story

In a 13-year period, I lost my older brother, my father, my husband, and my only son. Then, in 1991, I lost my only sister. Each of these deaths spurred me to embark on my spiritual quest.

When my 26-year-old brother, Mick, died of nephritis in 1959, he had been in the service, graduated from college, found a special girlfriend, and was just ready to embark on his life. However, he became ill and crossed over just ten days later. At the time, I was a senior at San Francisco State College, getting my teaching degree and dating Jerry Shea, who later became my husband and father of my three daughters and one son. I was taking a full load of classes in college and, living in different cities, we only met up once a week.

I had no car so I had to depend on the buses. After my brother Mick died, the only quiet time I had in my busy life was on those buses to and from school, and I always took advantage of this time to say my rosaries for Mick. Often, during my quiet moments together with Jerry, I would feel Mick's presence strongly, but as close as Jer and I were, I didn't mention this even to him. In fact, I'd never even heard of such a phenomenon. However, Mick's presence continued to grow in strength, but not being evolved enough at the time, I didn't realize that he might have been trying to send me messages. I'd never heard the word "meditation," but if I'd known, I would have quieted myself to listen. Sensing his presence was extremely distressing, and I became quiet, withdrawn and not as fun-loving as I'd once been. Poor Jerry couldn't figure out why and we came close to breaking off our relationship. This was my first clairvoyant experience, and Mick's presence has stayed strongly with me ever since.

Jerry and I married in 1960 and, in 1961, had our first child, Laura Marie. When she was 16 months old, we had our only son, Stephen Michael. Stephen came three weeks early, but he still weighed six pounds. He had blond curly hair and looked strong and healthy, but was born with mucus in the lungs. Only by wearing a mask and a gown were Jerry and I able to hold him, and then only a few times.

I wasn't told about his condition until his first scheduled feeding, and then learned that he had only a 50/50 chance of making it. When he crossed over just three and a half days later, my world crumbled again. It was hard for me to grasp, and before I was over the shock of his condition, he had already crossed to the other side.

Spirits like Stephen come to earth for a short time, living only hours or days after their birth, but come with a specific purpose. They arrange this early transition before they ever come to earth. These highly evolved spirits do not need the development that would result from a longer earth life. Their deaths provide challenges that help their parents and siblings grow. Their short duration on the earth plane is a great gift of love to the rest of us. There are no "accidents," and if it wasn't part of a soul's path, it would not go through the illness, accident or death.

Know that everything you are experiencing is in some way necessary for you to move to your next level of growth. Go into meditation and ask to see the "bigger picture." Learning from each experience in your life helps you to get beyond that experience.

I felt Stephen's presence after his crossing, but not as strongly as Mick's. Laura, too, has felt Stephen's presence very strongly all of her life. In fact, when she was three years old, we were sitting on the front porch and suddenly she pointed and said, "There's Stephen."

I saw nothing, so she described him, "He has blond curly hair and big blue eyes. He's wearing a red blazer jacket with gold buttons and is this tall." She indicated a height as though he was about two years old, the age he would have been had he lived.

I thought it was sweet that he'd dressed up to visit his sister, and I've always felt that he is planning to come back one day as Laura's son.

In 1969, my father had his first heart attack. Then in 1970, my whole world fell apart when he died of heart failure soon after his second heart attack. He was a fun-loving, warm, compassionate, loving person who gave me confidence in myself, and taught and showed me unconditional love. I was totally devastated with my father's death, and cried and prayed a lot.

When my father made his transition, my middle daughter, Barbara, was six years old. I took my three daughters to their grandma's house a few hours after their grandpa crossed over. Barbara walked right up to her grandma and held out her little hand. Unbeknown to me, she was holding the prized nickels from her piggy bank. She looked straight into Mom's eyes as she offered the nickels. She said nothing; her sad eyes said it all. Sometimes we adults are so involved with our own grief that we overlook the grief our young ones are feeling but are not yet able to express.

Sometime before Dad's death, I'd had my first psychic reading, in which, for the first time, I heard a sound that spirits can make, like someone snapping fingers. The psychic looked towards the sound and said, "Thank you."

Little did I know that, a short time later, when Dad died, I would hear this sound often. It always happened when I prayed for him. I'd feel his presence really strongly and hear the "click." Skeptics might say that this sounds like a house settling (it does), but it happens in the middle of the room. Often, I felt my Dad's presence so strongly that I thought he would materialize.

I wanted to share this moving, spiritual experience with my husband, Jerry, but I kept putting it off, afraid that he might ridicule the idea. Although he was very evolved, he was an engineer and tended to think more in black-and-white terms than I did. I finally got the chance one evening when the girls were settled in bed and we were both sitting at the kitchen table. I explained to him how I had heard these spirit sounds at a psychic reading, and then when I was praying for Dad.

Predictably, with his technical background, Jerry said, "Well it's probably just the sounds of the house. I have a hard time believing that a spirit could make that type of sound." So, desperate to have him believe what I knew to be true, I looked upwards and said out loud, "Okay, Dad, show Jerry how you can make that sound." Suddenly, the kitchen was filled with a cacophony of clicking sounds. Jerry jumped up from his chair and said, "Okay, okay, I believe."

Shortly after Dad's death, my sister, Mom, and I used to get together every Tuesday night to meditate. By then, I'd heard the term "meditate," although we knew nothing about getting into an altered state of consciousness. I simply closed my eyes, tried to make my mind a blank and visualized a blank blackboard. In this way, I started seeing spirits, especially family members who had crossed over to the other side. I realized then just how thin the veil is getting between the physical world and the spirit world. I also realized that I could get messages from the spirits, usually in the form of thought but often as though it was a movie. When they were emphatic about something, I would see things in large print, and often "heard" messages.

General ideas can be transmitted more readily than specifics such as names and dates. Most transmissions are sent as pictures and then I must translate the vision into words using my own vocabulary, ideas and beliefs. Through this early work with spirits who had crossed over, I came to know, without doubt, that mind and personality survive beyond death. I realized also that the more you mentally "talk" to your loved ones who have crossed over, the more you open your channels and the easier it is for them to communicate telepathically with you.

In 1971, my husband had his first heart attack. To my horror, in 1972, he died in my arms with his second heart attack, aged only 36. Just the night before, we were sitting out on our patio and he said, "We really have a lot to be thankful for, we have a happy marriage, three wonderful children, and we just put a down-payment on our dream house in Saratoga. I can't imagine what else anyone our age could ever hope for." He died in my arms the next night. I felt like someone ripped out my heart.

The day after he crossed over, most of his family and mine came to my house. As our house was quite small, his sister slept on his side of the bed. I woke up in the middle of the night to her sitting straight up in bed screaming, looking up above the bed. I saw nothing, but she'd woken up to see Jerry standing over me. (He was probably wondering why his sister was on his side of the bed.) While she was screaming, he told her, "Knock it off or you'll wake up Marge." With that, she screamed even louder. Trust me, she woke me up.

You often hear of people experiencing the presence of a loved one at the moment of death, almost as though the departing one had a rush of adrenaline at the moment of crossing. Some, like Jerry's sister, report actually seeing them. These spirits come to say "good-bye" to their loved ones.

That same night, a couple of my brothers were sleeping on couches in the living room, and they heard Jerry walking up and down the hallway. It unnerved them so much that one of my brothers went out to his car and got his gun. I guess he was planning to shoot my poor, dead husband!

At the time of Jerry's death, our oldest daughter, Laura, was 11 years old and in the sixth grade, Barbara was 7 and in the second grade, and Erin was 5 and hadn't yet started school. They were confused and devastated with his death. Death is a difficult concept for an adult, but it's incomprehensible to a five-year-old, especially when it's her daddy. When I told Erin that her daddy had gone to heaven with God during the night, she said, "You mean I'll never see him again?"

A day or so after the funeral, my three girls were watching television and I went out into our backyard. I was walking around, praying and crying over Jerry, and I didn't hear Erin come out of the house. Suddenly I felt her little hand slip into mine. She said nothing; she just intuitively knew my grief. At that moment, I knew that one of the many reasons she came back to earth was to help support me emotionally through the tremendous grief I was going through. Don't underestimate children, that's often where we'll draw our greatest strengths.

Vanishing Veil

I chose to protect my three daughters from viewing their father's body and from attending the emotionally intense funeral. I have never regretted that decision. All of their memories of their dad are of him alive, well and full of fun.

Barbara didn't immediately mourn her dad outwardly. About three and a half months later, however, a stray cat adopted us just before giving birth to a litter. Barbara in particular loved those kitties. When it was time for them to be weaned from their mom, I placed an ad in the newspaper, offering them free to a good home. When the last kitty was being taken from our home, Laura, my oldest daughter, came running to me saying that Barbara was laying face down on the carpet in the small space between her bed and the wall, and was crying hysterically. I knew at the time that besides feeling a sadness over the kitties, Barbara was finally releasing her grief over the loss of her daddy. Interestingly enough, her older sister, Laura, (11 years old) knew intuitively that that was what was happening with her sister Barbara.

I became aware right after Jer's death of Barbara picking up on my energies. Whenever I felt stressed, especially when expecting either social or business company, she would quietly ask me what she could do for me, what she could clean, or how she could help me.

Laura, as the oldest, had a very special "storybook" relationship with her dad. Her adoration and love for him were boundless, and she would go out of her way to sit by him or hold onto his arm as they walked along. Their growing relationship made me want to burst with happiness and love as it reminded me of my special relationship with my own father. After her dad's death, she became a rock of strength for me, always trying to anticipate my needs. In a split second, she went from being my oldest daughter to my best friend and companion. Laura is a very old soul, who was born old. She has always had an "all-knowing" quality about her. I drew a lot of strength from her in my grief and still do.

Despite all the deaths I had to endure, I was blessed with three highly-evolved daughters who never gave me a minute of grief. In fact, just the opposite; all three are my best friends, and we have an extremely deep spiritual bond.

With Jerry's crossing, I realized that the soul knows when it has accomplished what it came here to do. He came to help me to have and briefly raise our three wonderful daughters, and he waited for me to feel financially secure before making his transition.

I feel strongly that before they die, people know subconsciously that their time is near. It wasn't Jerry's nature to initiate games or outings with the children, yet the weekend before he crossed over, he suggested we take the girls to play miniature golf. It was a fun evening; I fell into one of the ponds and we all had a great laugh over that. Just hours before he died, he'd suggested a family game of croquet and then bike riding with the girls after that.

I was in the toy party plan business for 25 years, and a few months before he crossed over, I came home late from giving a toy party to find him sitting in the dark listening to classical music. He had tears in his eyes and said, "I've never done enough of this!"

On the subconscious level, I was intuitively picking up on what was happening. Driving home one night after giving a toy party, I heard on my car radio a song about growing old together. I started crying so hard that I couldn't see and had to pull over. I knew at that moment that we wouldn't grow old together.

Our 12th anniversary was April the 23rd. We celebrated the occasion with a wonderful dinner with two old college friends who shared the same anniversary. When we arrived home from dinner, Jer noticed on the table a copy of *Redbook* magazine, whose cover advertised a feature article: *Knowing What To Do When Your Spouse Dies*.

"You really should read that article," he said.

"Don't be silly," I retorted, even though I'd already read it. In fact, at that moment, I realized that I'd bought the magazine just because of that article. He then went to bed and I stayed up crying uncontrollably, knowing he would go soon and realizing that he also knew on the subconscious level.

It's important to understand that he was in great health then, or so we thought. The week before, we had put a down payment on our dream house in Saratoga. Before doing this, Jer went for a physical exam as a precautionary measure because he'd had a heart attack the year before.

The doctor told him, "If I didn't know better, I'd say you'd never even had a physical problem." Jer was dead one month later!

My channels truly opened up wide after Jerry's crossing. I went to the funeral parlor by myself to view his body for the first time. When I walked into the vestibule of the funeral parlor, a posted sign read, "Jerry Shea: Room A; Harry Jones: pending."

I heard Jerry, who'd always had a tremendous sense of humor, say, "I wonder if poor Harry knows he's pending?"

I laughed right out loud at the image of poor Harry sitting at home having dinner with his family not knowing he was "pending." As I walked up the aisle that seemed to never end to view Jerry's body, I felt him walking beside me with his arm around me.

After his rosary, family and friends came back to the house. The living room was jammed, and at one point, I glanced in from the kitchen and saw Jerry mingling with the crowd with a glass in his hand, laughing and visiting with them. He always loved a good party, but at that moment he looked confused. This was when I realized that when we cross over quickly, we're confused for a while, and often don't realize that we've been through the transition.

Looking back, I realize that it was my intuition that made me slip away from the group and go quietly into the back yard and mentally tell him, "Jer, you died and that's why no one is communicating with you. It's time for you to go to the Light."

People who have slow deaths are preparing themselves mentally for the transition, so they adjust much faster on the other side. Those who cross quickly—whether from accident, war, heart attack, murder, or whatever—often drift around on the astral plane wondering why no one's paying attention to them. They often go to work and continue on with their daily routines, not realizing what's happened to them.

Jerry was by my side to comfort me at his own funeral. Afterwards, I felt that I'd be nervous in my house with just my three young daughters and no other adult. I'd been brought up in a family with five brothers and a sister, so I'd always had others close to my age around in the evening hours. But, whenever I felt lonely or started to feel nervous, Jer and/or Dad would make the clicking noise to reassure me that I wasn't alone. I felt I had to be strong after his death and not break down too often in front of my girls since they were so young. After they'd gone to bed though, I would sit in my favorite chair and look at his picture and pray. More than not, I'd break down and cry. Again, I would feel his presence as he put his arms around me. I could distinguish his spirit sound from Dad's. Jer's was louder.

I got very clear messages and encouragement from Jer. I felt his mind touching mine. His words would often just drop into my thoughts, words I knew did not come from my consciousness. It was as though I had a celestial telephone. His death opened up a whole new world of awareness for me, and my level of consciousness rose rapidly as I constantly talked to my departed loved ones. I realize now that the more you do that, the more you're opening up your channels, and the easier it is for them to come through to you. They truly enjoy making these contacts, if for no other reason than to let you know that they haven't left you. Again, the veil between the two worlds is so very thin. Our lost loved ones want to reassure us that they are happy, well, and at peace. But, so often, we are too distraught to be open enough to hear them.

On the day my oldest daughter, Laura, graduated high school, my middle daughter, Barbara, graduated from junior high school. It was a hard day for all of us as this was the first really momentous occasion for us after Jerry's crossing. So, despite the tremendous pride that I felt, I was sad for my daughters whose dad wasn't there to share their special day with them. I felt his presence strongly all day, however, despite all the distractions with the festivities.

After Barbara's ceremony, one of my brothers started to focus his camera to take a picture of Barbara, me, and her sisters. Looking

17

through the viewfinder, he was completely unnerved to see Jerry, proud as can be, standing in the middle of our family group. This brother isn't into metaphysics at all, so this incident proves that this can certainly happen to anyone, even more so if you're open to it. He was so shaken by this experience that he was unable to attend Laura's high school graduation later that same day.

So know that our loved ones never really leave us. And, they're always there for our big occasions. They're only a thought away. It's just frustrating, for us and them, that we can't see them as readily as they can see us.

Almost 20 years after my husband, Jerry, made his transition, my family had another devastating blow. On a Friday morning, my sister, Pat, started feeling sick, although just the Saturday before, she was fit and healthy, and had danced up a storm at her son's wedding. She went to bed afterwards with "flu-like symptoms," and told her husband on Saturday morning that she should go to the clinic when it opened. Instead, he insisted that she go to the emergency room. As he put her into a wheel chair to wheel her into the hospital, she went into a coma from which she never recovered. She died in the middle of the night from gram streptococcus.

It's still hard for me to believe she's gone. Pat left a husband and five children, one of whom had just started college, with the youngest still in high school. I saw Pat at her own funeral mass, sitting on the altar railing just taking everything in. The many priests in attendance and the packed church were a beautiful tribute to her life. Sporadically, she would go over and put her arms around her children and husband.

My level of awareness had increased tremendously between Jerry's death in 1972 and Pat's in 1991, so I was able to communicate with her immediately after her crossing. I actually visit with her much more now than during the last years of her life on earth, when we were both very involved with our own families. While it's devastating to lose a loved one, learning to communicate with them telepathically helps greatly to get over the loss.

I started seeing my departed loved ones on a regular, often daily, basis. I would walk into a room with two or three people and see half a dozen spirits. It was distracting, to say the least, but I couldn't talk to anyone about it because most people would have felt I wasn't dealing with a full deck. I knew I was, however, so I just kept it to myself.

Soon after Jerry's death, I was in bed praying for him and Dad. I heard both of them call my name. Dad called me "Margie," and Jer called me "Marge." For some reason, this is much more difficult for them to do than making the spirit sound. I've only heard a spirit call my name about four times since then. Once was Una, my guardian angel, when I was up at Mt. Shasta writing this book, and once when Dad called it when I fell asleep at the wheel of my car.

In the early 1970's, I started giving readings for family and friends. The spirits would use me as a channel to communicate with a loved one left behind on the earth plane. Then, in the late 1970's, I began reading professionally. I didn't advertise, feeling that if someone was meant to hear about me, they would. For the first few years of reading professionally, I saw only spirits of my clients' family and friends who had crossed over. If they didn't have anyone close who had departed, I'd see their spirit guides and guardian angels and receive messages from them. After about eight years, there was a shift. Besides seeing my client's deceased family and friends, I found that I was also seeing the higher self or the God within (the soul) of people who were still alive and well in the client's life. That proved to be very useful because all of us say things at times that we don't mean, but our higher self (our God within) says only what we really mean.

Before a reading, I meditate, asking that I'll be accurate and that I'll receive only what's right and good for the client to know. I ask that I don't get anything negative unless it can be changed by prayer. I don't feel anyone comes to a psychic to hear about deaths. Every now and then, however, I've gotten a death, but it's always someone who the client already knows is dying and that person's higher self comes to say, "It's okay, I'm ready to go."

I'm also able to see spirits when doing telephone readings. I see them as easily as if the person was sitting in the room with me. It got to the point that, for many years, I saw more spirits than I saw physical bodies. I finally made an agreement with them that I didn't want to see them unless I closed my eyes or unfocused them (I usually close them), and the spirits complied.

When the spirit of a loved one who has crossed over comes in, I describe him or her (I don't usually get names). To verify who the spirit is, I have the client say the first name of who they feel it is. The spirit will then nod yes or shake no. The spirit then will often attune to my energy, intermingling their energies with mine, and I'll "feel" how they died. This is one of many ways for them to convince my client that it is truly them. For example, if the person died of a heart attack, I'll literally feel sharp pains in my chest.

Recently, when giving a reading for a male client, the first person I described was his cousin, with whom he'd been very close. After describing his cousin, I sensed he'd had a drinking problem while on the earth plane and that he was killed instantly in a car crash because he was drunk. I physically felt my own chest and head being crushed. This was correct.

For me, the experience when contacting spirits is more like listening to music than listening to a conversation. A telepathic link is formed between us, and the raw essence of the idea is instilled within me. Words in this state are secondary. The spirits may simply want to show themes to me so I can describe them to their loved one. Sometimes there's no message at all. The spirits' messages usually contain words of love and reassurance such as, "Don't worry. I'm all right."

If people were quiet while alive on the earth plane, they are still quiet on the other side, and vice versa. Often the client will exclaim, "That was exactly how he used to talk," or, "That was one of her favorite expressions." Maybe the spirits give me just a smile, a tear or the clicking noise so that their loved one will know when they're around them. Or their loved one often "feels" their presence, even feeling their touch. I act as a "funnel," so to speak, for their sounds or touches. Once a client hears or feels the spirits, and I'm there to explain the sound or sensation, then the client's channels are open for him or her to continue making this sort of contact. Often the client has already felt or heard something similar but had no idea what or who it was.

Like people, animals continue to exist in another dimension, and stay close to the people who loved them. I have often seen and described a client's deceased cat sitting on his or her lap, or a beloved dog on the floor beside the chair.

Dying is very much like being born. When you come into this world, you travel through the birth canal to a place where the lights are suddenly bright and people who love you wait to welcome you. The same process happens at death. At the end of the dark tunnel is a bright light, and your friends and relatives on the other side of the veil joyously welcome you.

Our loved ones, whether they be deceased family or friends, spirit guides or guardian angels, are always watching out for us. When my father firmly called my name when I fell asleep at the wheel of my car, he saved me from a head-on collision. It obviously wasn't my time to cross over. That happened soon after I was widowed, so I'm sure my three daughters didn't need the added trauma of having their mom in the hospital or the morgue.

Another time, after I'd finished giving an evening seminar and visiting with my clients, I started home over the Santa Cruz Mountains extremely late at night. About halfway to the remote summit, I noticed that my gas gauge was on empty. I called on my husband, Jerry, and asked him to push me over the mountain. I literally visualized him pushing the car. Once over the summit, I tried a couple of exits hoping to find a gas station open, but to no avail. I made it all the way home. I've requested his help several times since, and have never run out of gas since he crossed over. He was very protective of me when on earth, and still is.

Call on your guides and angels when you need them. They'll be there for you. Your guardian angel or guide is often a close friend or relative who has crossed over. Your guide is always there to love, encourage, and support you. Guides are entities who are highly evolved and skilled at transmitting energy from their dimension into ours.

Because we are currently in a very important transition time for the earth, many high guides are present and want to assist us. Learn to meditate and tap into that guidance that is available to all of us. When you meditate, you build a bridge to the higher realms. Edgar Casey, the all-time great medium of the century, once said, "Prayer is talking to God, meditating is listening." We need to do both. Through meditation you can easily make contact with your loved ones.

Know that you're not alone. Spirits on the other side and your own higher self on this side are always there to support you. However, they would be violating your free will if they guided you without you first asking for the help. So, you must remember to ask for guidance, then always go with your first thought, knowing that it was given to you by your guide. After that first thought, your own mind gets involved and starts analyzing. So, ask for guidance and then go with the flow.

Don't try to make something happen; allow it to happen. Entities from the other side aren't limited to our three dimensions, or even to our time, so their knowing is more comprehensive. "Ask and you shall receive."

My life has taken many exciting turns, and while not all have been upward, every single experience has taught me something valuable. We all come to earth to learn unconditional love for ourselves and everyone in our lives. We're also here to grow spiritually. We do this by magnetizing relationships and situations into our lives to learn from. These lessons can be either stepping stones or stumbling blocks. It is up to you whether you want to learn through joy, or through pain and struggle. But so often, we tend to grow faster and go within more when we're in pain. Personally, I'm a fast learner and will yell, "Help!" to my guides if ever I have an onslaught of emotional pain. When you're in a situation and you feel like you're in quicksand, go into your meditative state, call on your angels or guides to show you the "bigger picture" (i.e., what you are to be learning), and then learn it so you can get on with your life.

Work on the other planes of reality is as valued as our work is on earth, and spirits choose what they do on the other side. We take our interests, our strengths, and our skills with us when we cross over. For instance, after crossing over, many doctors help to work on cures with others in the medical field. Once they find a cure, they simply use telepathy and transmit the cure into the mind of someone who is on the earth plane.

I have a teaching degree. I taught fourth grade and then did substitute teaching, with a focus on special education. Then I moved into the toy party plan business for 26 years and taught adults motivational techniques. I now teach adults and children to open up to their own powers within and to see that there's a lot more beyond the three dimensions that seem to limit so many. I'm sure I'll continue to do my spiritual teaching after transcending.

At the time of death, you can either remain close to earth or move on to the level to which your spirit has grown and is most comfortable. However, most spirits choose to remain on earth for a short time to help comfort and heal their loved ones they have left behind.

Realize that the more knowledge you acquire here on earth, and the more you grow spiritually, the further and faster you'll progress on the other side. Growth is a never-ending process, and you continue to evolve to higher levels of consciousness even after crossing over to the other side. And hopefully, reading some of my case studies will dispense any fears you may have about dying.

I recently had a near-death experience (NDE). It came at the lowest emotional point in my life. I felt sharp pains in my chest (I had a minor heart attack many years before, shortly after my husband died), and I passed out (fortunately, I was lying down). I didn't see the dark tunnel with the light at the end that so many experience with their near-death experience, but I did feel a deep serenity and oneness with the universe. I realized I had no physical limitations. I also noticed that the colors were very intense.

I met my father, my brother, Mick, and my husband, Jerry. We were sitting under a tree at the top of a beautiful green hill covered with multicolored wild flowers. I felt their unconditional love for me and an overwhelming sense of peace and well-being. I knew that I didn't want to return to earth, but they told me I hadn't finished what I came here for. As we talked, Lisa, my granddaughter who was about two years old at the time, appeared on the other side of the veil with me. It was night time, so she was astral flying, which most of us do every night while we sleep.

We usually cross over at night to visit loved ones or to connect up with our guides and guardian angel. Sometimes we just travel around, which is why we often have a sense of *déjà vu* when we go some place. These *déjà vu* feelings could also be caused by a past life. We may remember this astral flight as a fragmented dream in the morning, but usually we don't remember it at all. Before we go to sleep at night, it's good to ask to remember what we do or where we go at night, then keep a pad and pencil by the bed so we can write it down upon awakening, before it floats out of our consciousness.

When Lisa appeared on the other side, she was flying through space with outstretched arms and her hair flying, saying, "Don't go, grandma, don't go."

At that moment, I decided to return, but before I left for home (earth), the Blessed Mother joined our group and merged her energies with mine. It was as though we became one. The unconditional love I felt emanating from her was overwhelming. Since that experience, whenever I'm down emotionally, she'll take me in her arms and rock me slowly in her loving embrace as a mother would rock her baby. The feeling of her unconditional love is indescribable.

Case Histories and Concepts

When starting to write this book, my intention was to have it be a comfort to everyone who has ever lost a loved one. I wanted to get the concept across that death is simply a transition that we go through, not a permanent loss. It's hard for someone to doubt the validity of life-after-death after coming to me and having me describe in detail their loved ones who have crossed over. It's comforting and healing. A soul's spiritual progress depends on the cycle of repeatedly coming to the denser energies of the earth plane, and then returning to the spirit world.

Then, after getting into the writing, I thought it would be interesting to include a cross-section of readings. Many of my readings lead to regressions, and some lead to clearings. Sometimes regressions and clearings are necessary to see how all the puzzle pieces fit together.

Past Lives and Regressions

We are souls reincarnating, life after life, slowly progressing in our evolutionary path towards God.

Your past lives are recorded in your cellular memory, and these memories are affecting you right now. You are the direct result of all your past programming from all of your lifetimes.

We carefully plan each incarnation. We choose our gender, parents, nationality, and astrological sign. However difficult the circumstances are in your family, you chose them for a reason. Being regressed through hypnotherapy enables you to see the "bigger picture."

Unless we learn from our mistakes, we are destined to repeat them. We need to break the patterns in our lives. Often these patterns are brought over from other lifetimes. This is why regressions are so essential in healing ourselves, for understanding where and when your fear originated enables you to "own" it and then let it go. Until then, it controls you without your conscious awareness. Past life regressions can also trigger dramatic changes in a person's present life.

I often regress my clients into early childhood to help them to unblock something they didn't want to think about or didn't know how to handle at the time. Instead, they "stuffed" it inside. Often just going back to the source is enough to release the problem, but sometimes a "forgive-and-release" process is necessary.

For example, a client of mine would drive literally hundreds of miles out of his way rather than cross a bridge. He was a salesman in an area where to be efficient, he needed to cross a multitude of bridges, so this was a tremendous hardship. After psychically ascertaining that this fear did not come from this life, I regressed him to a past life. He saw that he was driving across a bridge with his two very young children, became distracted, and drove off the bridge into deep water. He drowned trying desperately to rescue his two young children, who also drowned. One of his young ones in that life is his wife in this life. She, too, refuses to go near water in this life. Simply taking him back to the "cause" and having him see that his fear of bridges is from the past and not a premonition of pending doom allowed him to conquer it.

During a reading with another client, I flashed back to a past life where she died in a fire. After the reading, she told me, "My fear of fire is so overpowering that I can't even strike a match." When I regressed her, she discovered that, in five lives, she had died from fire, including one in which she was buried alive in hot lava from a volcano. No wonder she couldn't light a match. After the regression, the fear was gone!

If you've always wanted to go to a specific state or country, it's probably because you've had a quality life there. Since I was a young child, I've always loved pictures of lighthouses, always been drawn to the water, and always wanted to see the state of Maine. My second husband and I went back East to see the fall colors a few years ago.

We started out early one morning in Maine to find a lighthouse. Finally, after a frustrating search, we found one in Portland, Maine, long past midnight when the area was deserted. This was obviously intentional because I cried uncontrollably when I saw it. Through my tears, I had detailed flashbacks to when my father in this life was my father in that life, too, and once again showed me unconditional love. No wonder I picked him as my father again! Then, driving away from the area, we passed a small cemetery, and I knew our bodies from that lifetime were buried there.

Past life regressions reveal any karmic ties you have with loved ones and why, when you meet people for the first time, you immediately like or dislike them. You may have been happily married to them in the past, or they may have made your life miserable. Or say you have a sleep disorder, you may have been molested or murdered in your sleep and carried it over from a past life. When you find the cause, it's very often the end of your problem. That's what's meant by the term "cause and effect."

Clearings

At death, the consciousness floats above the lifeless body. Shortly after that, it moves through a dark tunnel with the God-light at the far end, beckoning to it. Friends and family are in the God light to greet the person crossing over.

Sometimes, the spirit becomes earthbound. In the worst case, it finds itself in complete darkness. Such a spirit is in the lower astral plane. This plane is near the surface of the earth. This entity may decide to stay in its previous home, or go to a favorite bar, or remain in the hospital after death, or in the cemetery where its body was buried, and occasionally, it will "jump" into the body of a nearby living person.

Studies indicate that one person in 12 is "possessed". Most entities that "possess" aren't "evil," however. Usually they're just clinging to another being for help. But, they can and do control the activity of their host. In general, a possessing entity is in a low spiritual state of mind and can only bring harm to the invaded host's body.

Why does it happen? If the entity is not spiritually evolved, it loves to continue to feel the earthly emotions. An unevolved entity of little spirituality doesn't readily give up his or her attachments for material things or pleasures when he or she crosses over. While on earth, if discarnate souls were bonded to the world through greed, drugs, alcohol, smoking, and other earthly addictive behavior, they find it difficult to move on into the spirit realms and often become earthbound. They often don't recognize the energy and light that pulls us toward God. These spirits stay on earth until they learn to let go of the world. Or, in some cases, they merge their energy with a person on earth who has their old earthly habits.

If you have any of these addictive habits, you're opening yourself up as a perfect target to host an addictive soul who has crossed over. In fact, you're almost defenseless against an intruding spirit. A heavy drinker on the earth plane, for example, may have as many as ten or more entities enjoying liquor through him. The host may want to stop the habit but is urged on by the intruding spirits.

Possession takes place more than most would like to think. In fact, it is estimated that approximately 85% of alcoholics and drug addicts are possessed. If you are in a hospital (as a patient or visitor) or visit a cemetery, you are truly exposing yourself to these entities, as there are many discarnate lost souls looking for a host. Be sure to keep your aura (personal energy field) sealed when under anesthesia as you are in a weakened state at that time.

I've often also seen that at death, departing entities will sometimes merge with a family member. The causes vary. Often they are simply fearful of the transition, or they may merge with a loved one in order to comfort them, or they may not want to leave them because of the close ties. This completely changes the person's life, as their deceased "intruder" brings along their mental, physical, and emotional blueprint. This is also why prolonged and profound grief can be harmful to you and the person you're grieving for. The bond of your grief my "lock" the other close to the earth plane indefinitely.

Often the human hosts will suffer dramatic emotional changes or become very depressed for no apparent reason. When they look into a mirror, they may see hate coming out of their own eyes or feel that someone else is looking out of their eyes. They may become upset for no reason. Your behavior pattern changes dramatically when an entity merges with you. If someone has been in a great depression for many years, he or she often houses several entities.

A clearing is needed when entities that have not made a successful transition to the other side step into the body of someone on the earth plane. Because of lack of knowledge or belief, or if they have some sort of addiction, some spirits are virtual prisoners of this earth.

Learn to connect with your lost loved ones through the spiritual world (meditation, telepathy, astral flight, automatic writing) rather than the cemetery. The cemetery is just housing their discarded body, whereas the whole being (character, intelligence, consciousness) is on the other side anxious to communicate with you through the spiritual realms.

As with a regression, after a clearing has been accomplished, the puzzle pieces fit together in the person's life, and clients who go through clearing often experience dramatic positive changes in their lives.

So, to augment the case studies on spirits coming through who have passed over, I felt it would also be helpful to add some stories of regressions and clearings so that you can see how it all fits together.

About the Case Histories

These presentations are actual texts from extensive recorded interviews that have been edited only for clarity and organization. It was helpful to have the recordings since I do my work in an altered state of consciousness and usually have no recall afterwards.

I find it enormously comforting to know that the mind and personality do indeed survive the death of the body, and that the death of the body is but a passing to a much freer and fuller life. I hope the following case studies will help you to find meaning in the cycles and stages of life, including the transition we call "death."

Case Histories

1. Joan

The first time Joan came to see me, it was five weeks after she lost Cory, her three-year-old son. She had been referred by someone at the Centre for Living With Dying. Her son had been at daycare in the cafeteria of an old, closed-down elementary school. The cafeteria was used as a multi-purpose room, and during daycare use, the large, metal, folding cafeteria lunch tables were stacked against the wall and locked. On the fatal day, someone had failed to lock one of them in. As Cory played in the room, the table fell on him and crushed his skull.

The daycare called her and said, "Cory has bumped his head, I think you should come."

While Joan was driving to the school, she saw the ambulance leaving, and knew, from the look on the face of the accompanying teacher, that it was not good. Joan knew that they were going to Valley Medical, which specializes in head and neck injuries. She became hysterical at that point, unable to move or drive her car. Two women helped her park and then took her to the hospital.

At the hospital, the doctors wouldn't tell her anything, despite her hysterically repeating, "Will I be able to take care of him?"

Eventually, the doctors came in and told her that little Cory had died instantly. At that point, her whole body just collapsed as she realized what had happened.

When Joan came to me, she told me nothing. I started off the reading by telling her that the spirits usually come in the order of importance that they are or have been in someone's life. Her mother came in first, with Joan identifying her from my description. Her message for Joan was simply, "I love you."

Next, her brother came in, and again, I described him perfectly. "He seems to be just coming in and messing up your hair."

"Well, my brother always does that to me. It's his way of showing affection. Now I know for a fact it's him."

"He wants you to know that he loves you very much and his heart is going out to you."

"Are your Mom and brother alive?" I asked.

Joan replied, "Yes, both are."

Just then, four more spirits came in, and I told her, "Everyone's telling you how much they love you. I feel they just want you to heal."

Joan fell silent again. Next, her grandmother showed up. "She has salt and pepper hair, more white than dark. She's a big woman. She's telling you not to be so sad, that you've got to work through this, to try and be strong. It's just going to take time. Now she's patting your hair and twisting it up in her hand, as though she's making a curl."

Joan was still playing Miss Skeptic, but that information about her grandmother got through to her. She knew exactly who I was describing and told me later that the hair curling had been the definite confirmation for her that the session was legitimate.

"Now I'm seeing a spirit standing beside you that I feel is your grandfather. He is also your spirit guide. He was really close to you while he was on earth. He's wearing a suit. Now that's odd; who wears a suit nowadays?"

"He *is* my grandfather. I named Cory after him. He always wore a suit."

"He's around you a lot. He's telling me to tell you that you just have to get over this, get through this."

I, of course, still knew nothing about Joan or who Cory was, and had no idea what he was talking about.

Joan then asked me, "Are all the spirits here that are in my life?"

"Not necessarily. Would you like to call someone in?" I asked.

"Yes, I would."

Just then, before she could reply, the spirit of a child entered the room. "Oh, someone just came in. He's real short, a child, with brown curly hair and big brown eyes."

At that point, for some reason, I started to take big deep breaths, and got very emotional. Later, Joan told me that she was thinking that it would have been only fair to tell me the story about Cory, but she didn't.

Then I found myself in pain and said, "My heart is hurting, my heart is hurting really badly." I started crying, sobbing, and couldn't get control. Cory was crying through me. His energies simply merged with mine, and he made an extremely emotional contact with his mom over being able to make this human contact with her.

"This is my son," Joan explained.

"He left you because of an accident, didn't he?"

Joan nodded and explained what had happened.

I was still trying to get my breath but managed to tell her, "Cory had to leave in order for you to become your own person."

"We were so close in the physical world that I know that's absolutely true. I learned to respect that, even though I don't care for it."

"Cory is showing me him pumping your bath oil into the bath tub."

The sudden gasp told me that this vision really startled her. "He used to get in trouble for doing that when he was alive, and it's happened a few times since he's been gone. In fact, this is one of the main reasons I've come to see you. I had to know if I was flipping out or if Cory could be doing this from the other side to attract my attention. I came to you because I've noticed things happening in my house. I felt his spirit was around, and I wanted to know if it was really him, or if I was just so overcome with grief that I was going crazy and making these things up. After he died, my house was so tidy that it really bothered me, because when you have a three year old, your house is never tidy."

Joan later told me that after learning that Cory was indeed around her, she'd leave the house and say, "Mess something up today, Cory." When she returned home, the dresser door would be open, or something would be moved on the dresser, or there would be the oil in her bathtub.

"My cat stares at the area where Cory used to sleep. The cat also sits at the window where I used to have Cory sit and watch me when I went to do the laundry. I definitely feel that he's still around."

"Cat's are very psychic or intuitive," I explained. "Your cat was probably seeing Cory."

"Cory is still earthbound and he doesn't understand why he has to leave and go to the light. That's very common when someone leaves the earth plane quickly. So, I suggest that you tell him to go into the light."

Joan later told me, "When he was alive, he would sit in the car's front seat with me, and he'd hold on to my right arm as I drove. When I left your house, I could feel him holding onto my right arm. I went directly to the cemetery. I'd previously placed a sparkler on his grave and it was gone. I took his hand and said, 'Come on, Cory, let's see if they threw it away.' We skipped all the way to the garbage can and the sparkler was still there. We picked it up and I remember waving it and he was still holding onto my other hand. I stood there and said, 'Now it's time for you to go to God. It's time for you to leave, for you to go to the white light.'

"I stood there for at least 10 minutes, saying, 'We will always be together. I will always love you, but you need to go sit with God, to learn from God and then you can come to visit me.' After that, he's never moved anything physical in my house again. I felt him letting go of my hand and I said, 'It's okay, God will protect you!' I feel his presence since then, but that's all. Nothing is physically moved.

Next, I told Joan, "As I go in on your energy, I feel you're really uptight. You're under way too much stress."

"Yes," she replied, "I'm pregnant."

"I'm seeing the father as being very tall and very thin. I feel he's quite immature, like he was a fun spark that came into your life to help you through some of your mourning period over Cory. I don't think you're going to marry him, Joan. I feel it's going to be just you and baby again. He came into your life so that you could conceive this baby."

"I think you're right," she admitted.

"I'm seeing you in a past life in Africa. You were black in your last life."

"Someone else has seen that too," she said, nodding.

"You were in a tribal type of situation. You were very insecure and immature. I'm seeing the other members of the tribe take your baby from you. It was taken from you more for what you didn't do than for what you did. It was neglect. You had a wonderful marriage. You became like one with your husband. Because of that, you neglected the baby, and you weren't accomplishing what you came into that life to accomplish. You came back this time determined to grow on your own, to be independent. You came back nervous about having too strong a relationship, knowing how all consuming it can be for you. Whenever you start to see a relationship becoming serious, you put out such fear, almost negative vibrations, that it frightens men away."

"Well, it's nice to know I was at least married in a past life," she said, smiling ruefully.

"You had a beautiful marriage in that past life. You never had any more children after that one was taken from you. There was no room in your life that time around for a child. You both decided that you needed to come back this time together so you both could grow and evolve spiritually, because you didn't in the last life. Cory was the man you were married to in Africa."

"Cory was half black in this life."

"Your essences were one. Your whole being was one. You knew you couldn't be married, but there was no way you wanted to go through a life without each other. He loved you so much from that last life that he agreed in this life to serve as a stepping stone for you and your spiritual progression."

"Do you see me ever marrying in this life?" Joan asked.

"You're going to find someone who's almost father-like towards you. A very loving, protective, nurturing man. He'll also have a lot of passion and compassion for you. I'm hearing that this will be good for you, as you never had a great relationship with your own Dad."

"That's right."

"He's going to be the father you would have liked to have had to lean on. You'll marry only once in this life, and be happily married. He's not going to sweep you off your feet, but he's going to be a wonderful person. He has a stout build. His hair is a little receded. He'll absolutely cherish you. I feel Cory is directing all this."

With that, the session naturally came to a close.

Two years after Cory's death, and following the birth of a daughter, Tamara, Joan returned for another session.

"I made an appointment with you this time for a clearing. I found out through you at my last reading that I've picked up a female spirit during one of my visits to Cory's grave at the cemetery. I try to go there once a week to bring Cory fresh flowers."

"Before we do this, let's go into your baby daughter's vibrations. As I go into Tamara, I keep wanting to frown. I feel very strongly that Tamara's the child that got taken away from you in that past life. She came into the world frowning, thinking you may not love her because of your strong love for Cory."

Joan laughed. "That's really interesting! She didn't smile for at least three months, and I was real worried that maybe I'd put this on her by thinking that, while I was pregnant, I could never love her as I loved Cory. I still feel Cory's around me, even though he doesn't make himself apparent through the physical world anymore. I think that is good, because I would tend to want to be with him, even knowing that I need to get on with my life and enjoy my daughter."

Armed with the knowledge of Tamara's concerns, Joan left the session ready to give her new daughter the loving attention she needed.

Comments on Joan

Joan's story is very moving. I don't believe that any of us can relate to losing a child—our own flesh and blood—unless it has happened to us. Even then, it's hard to relate because of the different circumstances and personalities involved. The one thing that we all have to realize is that, on one level or another, all parties involved agreed on Cory's untimely death. But it's hard to see the bigger picture when you're going through the grief connected to losing your child. That this was all planned is impossible to imagine while we are going through the grief period, but we all come here to learn lessons. It's through our lessons that we grow, and we can use our lessons as stumbling blocks or stepping-stones on our spiritual path. And, of course, most lessons we learn are through relationships.

In these sessions with Joan, a past life connection came through which made sense to Joan. No psychic can tell you anything that you don't know yourself on one level or another. In fact, often it's good to go to a psychic simply to have what you feel to be true confirmed by someone who doesn't know you.

Cory is an extremely evolved old soul. It truly is a rarity when a spirit can move physical objects. Once, when I was in the toy party plan business, I lost one of my demonstrator's contracts, and I needed to send it in to the home office that day. I looked and looked for it to no avail. So, I called on my spirit guide to help me, and the next time I walked into the kitchen, it was in the middle of the table. I know for certain that nothing else had previously been on this table, and I had definitely looked there before! I knew it was my father who placed the missing contract there. But as long as I've been aware of the fact that there's more than three dimensions, I've only seen items moved a few times, commonly hanging lamps swinging back and forth to attract my attention.

Cory's story is a great example of how a spirit stays earthbound for awhile following sudden death, even when, as in Cory's case, the spirit is very evolved. Many highly evolved beings want to be on earth at his time for the current dramatic increase in the level of consciousness. By taking his turn and then crossing over after barely three years, Cory was spiraled even higher on the other side.

Joan also mentioned her cat seemingly seeing Cory. Animals, especially cats, are extremely intuitive. Whiskey, my husband's black cat, used to love being in my living room during readings. As the spirits appeared, Whiskey would stare into what appeared to be thin air and spin rapidly around in circles, usually with his hair standing on end as if scared. I knew, however, that on one level, he enjoyed the energies. And he always wanted to be present when I gave seminars. Other than that, though, he was strictly an outdoor cat.

In Joan's case, she also needs to go through a forgive and release process; she needs to forgive whomever failed to secure that table, and she needs to forgive Cory for abandoning her.

2. Doris

Doris came to me for an appointment after her gay son was murdered by his lover. She had gone into a metaphysical store and picked up a paper called *Psychic Reader*. When she got home and read the paper, she saw my photograph and immediately exclaimed, "Wow, there's a lady who gets in touch with the spirits." She had been searching for someone with the ability to put her in touch with her deceased son. She told me later that for some reason, my picture kept coming up in her mind along with a strong urge to call me and make an appointment. Having not been in San Jose for a long time, she was wary of the heavy traffic and made an appointment for a phone reading. However, something told her that she had to be there personally, so she changed the appointment.

Doris was very nervous about coming to San Jose because it is such a large and busy city, but much to her surprise, she didn't get lost. In fact, she was led directly to my house. When she arrived, she told me, "I don't know what I'm here for, except that I've lost my son."

That was all she said. I went into trance and immediately, a young man appeared in the room. I described him to Doris, and she said, "That's a perfect description of Kirk, my son. Now I know why your picture made such an impression on me. Kirk directed me to you."

Having her son in the room with her, Doris got really emotional. And she was certain it was him because "there was absolutely no way you could have known what he looked like and you described him to a tee."

Kirk began by telling me, "I was gay," and then asked me to relay to his mother that, "You were the only one in the family that knew."

At that point, Doris really lost control of her emotions because this was correct, she told me between her sobs.

Kirk went on, "My lover who I lived with murdered me because of his intense jealousy."

Doris confirmed that Kirk had been murdered—good confirmation for me, since all she had said was that she had lost her son.

Kirk continued his story. "You were right, Mom, about that night. I'd confronted Cliff about all the unpaid bills."

I described the scene to Doris as Kirk showed me that Cliff was high on cocaine and alcohol. As Cliff became extremely violent, I could see that he was jealous of Kirk even though they were supposedly best friends. Cliff was jealous of Kirk's achievements and also the fact that Kirk had other friends.

I relayed to Doris as Kirk told me, "I considered Cliff the very best friend I'd ever had. I was both drawn and attracted to him, yet fearful of him. My instincts told me that Cliff would or could do me in. I was confused about myself, however, and I couldn't find my rightful place while I was there on earth. I was unhappy about who I was, and was trying to find myself. But, now I'm here, I've found myself and my true and rightful calling, which is helping other murder victims cross over. I stay with them through their sleep period and through their adjustment. This is my mission and I'm very happy about it."

Kirk went on to say, "And, Mom, your mission is to help the families of these victims. That's one of the reasons why I died the way I did, so that you could achieve your mission in this life. My death happened in order to give impetus to what you're supposed to do."

Another young man then joined Kirk. He had light blonde hair, and was tall and thin. I described him to Doris, but she said, "I don't know who you could be referring to."

Having more ground to cover, we let it go, but later, however, Doris told me, "You remember the young blond man you saw? That was Cliff, my son's murderer."

"Oh, what happened to him?" I asked.

"He was sentenced to life in prison with no possibility of parole."

"I'm getting some interesting information on the karma between Kirk and Cliff. I'm seeing Kirk as a heavy drinker in a past life, always getting stopped by the police and warned about drinking and driving. One evening, he was very intoxicated and ran down an older man in a crosswalk. The man, Cliff, died a slow, agonizing death.

"In this current life," I continued, "Cliff has an explosive temper, combined with the karma between them. But he wiped the slate clean by stabbing Kirk multiple times with a knife. Kirk's death was agonizing, but mercifully fast."

Next, a lady came in and I described her to Doris. "Is this your mother?" I asked.

"No, but the description fits my aunt who crossed over about two weeks ago."

"Yes, that's true," I said, "because she's smiling and saying, 'Yes.' Oh, and your son has his arm around her."

Just then, another woman joined them and I described her.

"That's my mom," Doris said, excitedly. "I know beyond doubt that it's my mom!" Doris was visibly shaken at this very emotional, moving, and touching experience of having so many relatives show up to greet her.

Then, Kirk said to his mother, through me, "I want to prove to you that I've been with you always. I'm very concerned about Derek (his brother). Derek feels that he's the one who should have crossed over instead of me. He feels like he's always been second best to me and feels guilty about being alive when I'm dead. He needs a lot of assurance and a lot of love."

Doris became even more emotional, and said, "I know that's true. Derek was 16 years old when Kirk crossed over."

Kirk continued, "Don't feel guilty, Mom, that you loved me more than my brother. It's because we have had a very deep bond. We were married in the last life we had together, and we had a very close and loving relationship. In fact, we've had many lives together. And please don't hate Cliff because this will only hold you back on your growth. Every time I come to you, you'll feel a tingling and a touch on your arms, shoulders, or face, like a spider-web."

After the session, Doris told me, "I often feel something like a spider's web on my face and I keep trying to brush it away. Also, my hair starts to stand up on the one side of my head and I feel a tingly energy. When this happens, I know that someone's with me."

When Doris came for a second reading, before she had even sat down, Kirk appeared. "He's here already," I told her. "His energy is very strong, he was here even before I called him. He seems anxious to make contact. He's telling me that you're contemplating filing a wrongful death suit against Cliff. He's telling you not to."

A woman entered at that point, and when I described her, Doris said, "That's my mother-in-law. She's just crossed over."

"She has her arm around your son, and she's telling me that she's happy to be rid of her worn out body. She says she's okay and very happy, and that she's grateful that you went over to her house the week before she died and told her about the after-life."

Doris later told me that this was true. She hadn't seen her in quite a while before that. Her mother-in-law told us, "I've been literally shaking my son, Robert (Doris' husband) by his shoulders to get his attention and I've been there with him very many times, but he's unaware of me because of his heavy drinking. I think Robert's on a self-destructive course. I wasn't aware of his excessive drinking until I died, or more accurately, I didn't want to believe it before, but now I know the truth."

At that point, I delicately ventured an observation. "I'm getting bad vibrations from Robert because he's in a bad space, and he feels a lot of guilt over Kirk's death because he feels he could have done more for him. But he shouldn't worry because Kirk is in a very high place."

Doris then asked, "How is Cliff doing in jail?"

"He is not liked in prison and is having a rough time. On some level, he feels he deserves this because of what he did to his lover."

Kirk chipped in at that point to say, "I'm concerned about Derek's health, Mom. You should take him in for a thorough checkup whether he wants to or not because he's too wound up and he has a lot of unexpressed emotions. He's under a lot of tension, and he needs to talk about it. He needs to release all his pent-up feelings, because everything has been too much for him."

I saw Derek and said, "He has a lot of jealousy regarding the attention surrounding his brother's death, and at the same time, he feels guilty about it. So much has happened and he's holding in too much."

Doris' Mom came through then and said, "I often got too caught up with the material side of life. I'm glad to see that you're not getting caught up in that trap, and I'm really pleased to see you progressing spiritually. I want you to know it's me, so I'm going to give you proof."

At that point, my neck began to hurt and I started to rub it. I told Doris, "For some reason, my neck is very stiff. And I'm having trouble catching my breath. My chest area feels tight and congested.

What did your Mother die of?"

Doris answered, "My Mom died of pneumonia, so actually you're having the same symptoms that she had when she was dying. She had terrible headaches that went down into her neck, plus hypertension and multiple strokes. But in the end, what she died of was pneumonia and that's why you're having so much trouble breathing."

Doris' mother continued, "Despite all the headaches you've been through, you still seem to smell the roses. You are putting everything into the right priority."

Then, Doris asked, "There's someone who seems to come into my bedroom, sit down on my bed, and wake me up. Who is it?"

"It's your son. He just wants to talk. He's a very strong spirit. I think it's because of the coming holidays (this reading was just before Christmas)."

Then I added, "Kirk wants you to know that he was meant to go and it was not an accident. It was really his time. He knows that it's been really difficult and hard for you, but says he'll be with you on Christmas. He's saying, 'You're going to feel my presence very strongly.' And he adds, 'I'm getting stronger and stronger and one day you'll see me.'"

Doris replied, "I haven't seen him yet, but maybe it's because I've been really low on energy. Can you ask Kirk if his brother, Derek, will ever see him, because he wants to badly."

"Kirk says, 'Although he wants to, Derek has his own walls around himself, so it's going to be very difficult for him. I don't think Derek will see me first. Mom, relax more; your nerves are too uptight. Listen, you will become very involved with people who are also victims and even become a pathfinder for these groups. You'll become a real inspiration to others who have lost a loved one.'"

Comments on Doris

It's always extremely difficult to lose a child, but to have one murdered, to have someone snuff out his or her life in a seemingly senseless act has to be one of the biggest challenges we can face while on the earth plane. This really tests our acceptance that on a higher level we agree to everything that happens in our life and that we co-create our lives.

Kirk conveyed to his mom through me that he felt he could accomplish more on his spiritual path by being on the other side of the veil. He also knew that his crossing would propel his mother onto her spiritual path.

Now, Doris' biggest and most challenging task is to forgive and release Cliff for taking her son from her. We don't have to condone, but we need to forgive before we can go on. Otherwise we become caught up in quicksand and can't move ahead spiritually. We need to look at this situation as the ultimate test. Doris wouldn't have agreed to go through something this horrendous if she wasn't a very highly evolved, old soul and knew she would take a quantum leap forward in her spiritual growth by agreeing to experience this.

Although we are truly all one with God, when everything is going right in our lives, we usually don't take the time to discover our God within. There's an old saying: "There's no such thing as an atheist in a foxhole," meaning, of course, that when we're frightened, hurt, resentful or in danger, we then turn to our higher self, our God within. We turn to prayer, we turn to meditation, and ask, even beg, for help.

Unfortunately, we tend to grow more through pain than through joy. There is most definitely a reason for forgiveness, for it cleans and heals your energy, or aura. Forgiveness is the key to inner peace because it is the mental technique by which our thoughts are transformed from hatred to love. We need to feel love enter our heart to help us to forgive all of our old hostilities, angers, resentments, and hurts of the past. By forgiving, you are giving up your old, negative past for a new, loving life. We need to forgive (not condone) everyone, including ourselves. We need to forgive ourselves most of all for wanting or needing various negative experiences in our life. Forgive yourself daily. This will free you to live in inner love and peace.

How can we possibly forgive someone for such a dastardly deed as murdering our child? One of the easiest methods I have found is to get yourself in an altered state of consciousness. You do this by sitting without crossing your arms or your legs—this allows the universal energy to flow through you.

Then start taking some deep abdominal breaths. Tell yourself and know that every time you inhale, you're breathing in peace, joy and unconditional love, and that every time you exhale, you're getting rid of all angers, resentments, stress, and stuck energy. So know that you're inhaling everything your body needs and you're exhaling everything your body doesn't need.

Do this for at least 10 breaths. Then visualize a large balloon, any color you choose, up in the sky. See the person you most need to forgive up in that balloon. Then see yourself go into that balloon with this person. Visualize the color gold all around this person. Gold neutralizes thoughts. Thought is energy. You don't want your bad thoughts about this person to hurt them—that just causes more karma between the two of you. Then, verbally let them have it. Say everything you've always wanted to say to them but have held back. If it feels good to you (even if you're not normally a physical type of person), see yourself hitting, punching, and kicking this person. This is very therapeutic as it helps to bring everything that you've been feeling, everything that you've been holding in, up and out of your body. We must get all these buried resentments up and out of our bodies, otherwise they'll manifest themselves in the form of physical illness.

Continue yelling, screaming, crying (whatever it takes) at this person for as long as it feels right to you. Then, when you're finished, visualize a beautiful ball of white light six to eight inches above their head—their higher self or their God within. Also, see a beautiful ball of white light six to eight inches above your head—your higher self or your God within. Have your God within forgive their God within. This way, you're not dealing with the personality or character of the person. No matter what they've done, we can forgive their God within, their soul.

Then, see yourself getting out of the balloon and leave the other person in the balloon. Visualize yourself standing in a gorgeous meadow. See this person in their balloon in the sky. Now visualize a string attached to this balloon, with the other end attached to your heart (or to your second chakra if you were sexually abused by this person). See yourself pick up a pair of scissors and cut the string. Feel the release as this person floats out of your aura and away into the universe.

Now see yourself facing yourself, visualize yourself walking into your own arms—feel your arms around yourself. Tell yourself you love yourself, that you're lovable, that you forgive yourself for wanting or needing that experience. Always conclude this exercise with a few affirmations, like, "The past is over, I am free," or, "The past has no power over me."

Another good time to do this forgive and release process is when you are walking or doing any sort of exercise. (Because of the deep breathing involved in exercising, you are in a natural, altered state of consciousness.) When I'm on my daily walk, I personally fill the sky with balloons! We definitely need to do this process more than once, especially when the hurts and resentments run deep.

Here is a shorter version which you can do literally hundreds of times a day—any time this person comes into your consciousness. Simply see ˀ cord between you and keep cutting the cord. This keeps them from draining your energy. In cases where you don't know what the perpetrator looks like, just visualize a person without a face. It's your intention that counts, not the face itself.

Forgive and release practices put us back in control of our lives. We cannot stay in a victim role, otherwise the resentments will literally eat away at you, in the form of an illness.

So, Doris not only needs to forgive and release Cliff, she needs to forgive and release her son Kirk for abandoning her. Their soul connection ran deep.

3. Natalie

Natalie came to me for quite a few readings in a short period of time, mostly due to relationship problems. Finally, when she called me for yet another reading, I said, "You know, Natalie, you wouldn't need so many readings if you'd let me give you a regression. In the regression, I'll take you back to source, to find out why you have this pattern of drawing men into your life who won't be permanent, or who will abandon you."

She agreed, and we set up the next appointment.

I took her back to early childhood in this life, even though she had told me that she didn't feel that her problems with men stemmed from her early childhood. However, Natalie was wrong. She was shocked by what came up for her. Not only did she remember but she also saw vivid pictures, like watching a movie. Here, in her own words, is what she experienced.

"When I went back to nine months old, I saw my father and started shaking with fear of him. So, Marge took me back farther to find out the source of this fear, in fact, to the day I was born. My mom was holding me and my dad was in the room with us. I started to cry because telepathically, I knew that neither of them wanted me.

"When I was seven months old, I was crying so my father tried to suffocate me with a pillow. My mom walked into the room and caught him, so he stopped.

"Next, I saw myself as a toddler, feeling like the world was against me. When Marge told me to go into my emotions, I sobbed for a long time. I couldn't see that I was doing anything 'bad' to warrant all the spankings I got.

"I saw myself as a two-year-old, climbing on a wood pile in our back yard. I fell and cracked my knee open. Besides the tremendous pain, there was blood everywhere, and the sight of it scared me to death. I just needed someone to hold me and tell me I'd be all right, but instead, my dad found me and beat me for climbing on the wood pile.

"We then went forward to age five. I saw my step-grandfather, Creighton, coming at me with what I called his 'snake.' I felt my fear, I heard myself in a toddler's voice crying, 'Go away, go away.' His assaults on me went on for at least three years. I would have thought that I would have remembered that happening to me at the age of eight, but the only thing I consciously remember is that I never liked grandma's new husband.

"Marge then led me through a forgive and release process. Soon after this session, I went back to my first husband who I had divorced many years before. This has been my longest relationship to date. He crossed over with cancer a few months ago."

Comments on Natalie

When I first met Natalie, she'd had at least three intimate relationships in the past five months. All three men had dropped her, which had a devastating effect on her.

Before I started the regression, Natalie assumed that she'd brought this relationship problem over from a past life. As I was putting her into an altered state of consciousness, I received the strong psychic impression that her problems stemmed from early childhood in this life. So, I followed my intuition and took her back in this life.

Her conscious mind kept telling her that she wanted a man, while her subconscious mind said, "You don't want a man. Look how men have treated you in the past." So, on the conscious level, she drew men in rapidly, but, because of her subconscious mind fighting her, she attracted men who wouldn't stay in her life for very long.

Just directing her to go into her emotions when she was a toddler and sobbing helped her to release. Crying is one of the most therapeutic things we can do for releasing garbage that we've stuffed inside ourselves from the past.

At the time of her regression, Natalie was in a mentally abusive relationship. She sent me a Christmas card and her return address took me by surprise. She lived on Creighton Street—her grandfather's name! Coincidence? I don't think so. The universe talks to us in many different ways. It was telling her she needed to deal with her past relationship with her step-grandfather, Creighton.

Now that she's single again, she needs to keep affirming to herself, (preferably when looking into her eyes in the mirror.) "I am loving and lovable," and "I deserve a loving, honest, fun, relationship, and I accept it now."

As with so many children, she had the repetitious thought, "There must be something really wrong with me," recorded in her memory bank. She needs to release that old programming and reprogram her subconscious mind.

She should make a list of her needs in a relationship and begin affirming those needs daily. Then read the list every day (be very specific) and say, "I release my needs to God."

Don't set limits. Say, "This or something better is now coming to me." Create a vision of what and who you want in a relationship, but leave the face blank—don't assume that you know him or her. Then hold that vision.

Next, put yourself in an altered state of consciousness by taking some deep breaths and progressively relaxing your body. Then visualize yourself with a partner doing everything you enjoy doing—playing golf, traveling, tennis, dancing, going for walks, or whatever.

The more detail you include, the faster you'll attract your next partner into your life. Even see yourself on the telephone calling family and friends, excitedly telling them that you've finally met your soul mate. Feel the excitement. The more emotional charge you put into your visualization session, the faster you'll draw in your permanent mate.

Remember the old saying: "Love is not about finding the right person; it's about *being* the right person." You draw to you what you are, not what you would want or like. So it's imperative to keep yourself in a positive space. Every time you say a negative word to or about yourself or make yourself wrong, your emotional body changes its vibration and your energy drops. You then attract to yourself people and events that resonate with this lower self-image, and amplify this drop in energy.

And one final point: Your desire for what you want must be stronger than your fear of having it.

4. Beatrice

Beatrice was at my monthly meditation group when I performed a group clearing. I told the group that if anyone didn't feel that they needed one, just send it to someone else.

She sent the clearing to her oldest son, Brandon, who is 25 years old and an alcoholic. This was interesting because it's often family members who do the possessing.

Beatrice later told me, "My first husband, Brandon's dad, and his father in turn are both alcoholics. When I started going in on Brandon, I felt that the problem was Phil's dad, (Phil is my second husband). Although I never met Phil's dad—he died in a barroom gunfight many years before I met Phil—I knew that he'd been an alcoholic. We lived in his house, and I'd always felt that his spirit was still in that house. We'd go over to visit Phil's mom when my son was younger, and Phil's dad's spirit apparently attached itself to Brandon, who started drinking at the age of eight. I didn't feel that he was a bad spirit, but that he just wasn't yet ready to go to the light and wanted to continue his drinking.

"Since the clearing, Brandon's drinking has stopped completely. He started going to church on Sundays and Wednesdays and attending Alcoholic Anonymous meetings. His friends are calling him 'Preacher Brandon.'

"He'd tried to stop drinking so many other times but to no avail. I feel he has licked his problem. It's now been sixteen months since the clearing. For the three and a half years that I've been coming to you, you always told me that there was a light at the end of my tunnel concerning Brandon. You were right! I don't remember when I've felt this happy."

Comments on Beatrice

Alcoholics and drug addicts more often than not have intruding spirits in them enjoying the liquor and/or drugs through their host. So even if these people want to turn their lives around, often their intruders spur them on to continue drinking and/or using other substances.

Anytime we drink, use recreational drugs, smoke, or go to a cemetery or a hospital, we are opening ourselves wide open to attachment by an entity.

5. Lynn

Lynn showed up for a session with me knowing nothing about her. As soon as the session began, a male spirit appeared and I described him to Lynn.

"That's my estranged husband."

"I see that you two are separated, but that you still have a lot to deal with around him. He is extremely negative due to his having a horrible childhood. I also see that he is physically as well as mentally abusive to you."

Lynn nodded in agreement.

I continued, "He also has a teenage daughter who is closer to you than she is to her father. I see you living in the house of an older woman, someone who is extremely negative and whose negative vibrations are going to adversely affect you if you don't move soon. I am seeing your ex-husband peering through your windows after dark." (Lynn later confirmed that she'd had to call the police about his peeping tom activities.)

I continued telling Lynn what I was being shown. "You should keep your car in a garage, otherwise he's likely to damage it in some way." A rueful Lynn later told me that she didn't listen and that her ex poured ten pounds of sugar into the gas tank. Needless to say, the car was ruined.

I next described a woman who came into the session.

"That's a perfect description of my mother. She's just crossed over."

I told Lynn, "Your mother is saying, 'I'm distressed because my home is being unnecessarily tied up in legal red-tape by an unscrupulous attorney. And I'm unhappy about the way your brother is handling the delay in the settling of my estate. Apparently, he is blaming this legal mess on you instead of the attorney. Also, your brother is cheating on his wife. I'm so terribly disappointed in him.' "

Lynn gasped and said, "That's amazing. You had no way of knowing that of the two of us, my brother was the apple of my mother's eye. That's why she was particularly disappointed in him."

Comments on Lynn

This case shows us that we do carry our concerns over to the other side of the veil. Lynn's mom was staying earthbound until her estate was finalized. Then she'd feel freer to go into the light.

Instead of letting her judgmental attitude over the estate bother her, Lynn and her mother would be better served by counteracting the whole situation with something positive and sending healing energy to him. If they did, the situation would automatically change.

In a situation like Lynn and her ex-husband, she needs to ask herself, "What is he projecting to me that I need to learn?" Patience? Forgiveness? It's hard to do that sometimes. It means we have to take responsibility for everything that happens to us, including when people "do it to us."

People are in your life to serve as mirrors for things you need to look at. If someone's awareness is very limited, you may be drawing that person to you to tell you that you need to increase your own awareness. As soon as you work on your own awareness, he or she will go away. They are there to tell you that you need to expand, but be careful not to give any of your power to them.

6. Ken

When he came to me for a reading, Ken was in the middle of a divorce from Nancy, to whom he had been married for six years. Ken and Nancy have a three-year-old son, Ben. They had been separated one other time for nine months when Ben was six months old.

Ken and Nancy now live in different cities, an hour's drive apart. Ken picks up his son and takes him to his place on his two days off every week. When he has to return Ben, it's extremely traumatic for both father and son. Ken lives in constant fear of losing his son.

Although Nancy tells him often how much she loves him, she has never been able to show her love for him and Ken complained that she was unable to sexually satisfy him. Before the divorce proceedings had started, Ken had gone back to her several times hoping, for Ben's sake, that she had changed and could and would show her love. However, Ken said that she remained cold to him.

Psychically, I saw that there was a strong past life connection between the three of them, and suggested a past life regression. This would also take him to the source of the seemingly unfounded fear of losing his son. Ken agreed.

I began with, "I ask Ken's higher self or his God within to take him into the past life that most affects the one he's in today."

Ken picks up the story:

"I live in Europe. My mother is cold, and a strict disciplinarian. I feel that she doesn't love me. My mother is Nancy, my wife in this life. My father is full of love and compassion. In this life, he is my kind, loving grandfather. I have only one sibling, a brother who is a few years older than me. We are extremely close. We get each other through the strictness of our mother. My brother is Ben, my son in my current life. I really look up to and admire my older brother. In my current life, I feel that, although Ben is only three years old, he is an old, old soul. I already admire some of the words of wisdom that come out of his mouth.

"One day, I come home to find my house has been bombed. I discover the bodies of my mother, father, and brother. I am distraught at the loss of my family. After the bombing, I go to live with my aunt, who is very loving towards me. She was the only grandma I knew in my current life. She lived only until I was four, yet I remember her fondly. That same aunt in my past life had one daughter. I've met her this time around and feel a strong bond with her.

"I never got over the bombing, and died of pneumonia and a broken heart at age twenty.

"I realize that the main reason I needed to marry Nancy in this life was so I could have Ben back in my life."

Comments on Ken

Again, as with every regression, the puzzle pieces fit together perfectly! Ken saw clearly why he is obsessed about losing Ben. He now knows it's not a premonition and can redirect all the energy he was putting into fear into positive loving energies instead.

The session also helped him to realize that Nancy was sincere in the fact that she loved him as much as she could, considering that she'd brought these emotions over from that past life. It's easier to forgive and release emotions connected to a past life than emotions connected to this life.

When Ken was reliving his moving in with his loving aunt after the bombing, and that she was his grandmother in this life until he was four, I picked up psychically that the spirit who was his aunt from the past and grandma in the present is his main spirit guide.

Frequently one of our guides is someone who loved us in either this life or a past life. It's comforting to know that they don't leave us!

7. Sarah

Sarah's parents brought her to see me. Her mother told me, "Ever since Sarah was an infant, she had always had nighttime fears and sleeping problems. She would often wake up in her crib in the middle of the night screaming in fear. She would be afraid to be left alone and would force herself to stay awake until she was sure she would be allowed to sleep in our room. As soon as she was able to move around on her own at night, we would often wake in the morning to find her curled up on the floor beside our bed. She would arrive silently sometime in the middle of the night and sleep peacefully at our side. Between the ages of two and four, she would often speak of seeing 'clowns' that scared her.

"When Sarah was two, she needed to have an operation to remove her adenoids. They were so enlarged that when she lay down to sleep at night, she couldn't breathe very well and wasn't getting enough oxygen. After the surgery, her nightmares increased dramatically. And despite the fact that she was now getting sufficient oxygen in her sleep, she was now snoring louder than most adults do. The doctors assured us that this was normal and would subside quickly. It never did. We could hear the sound of her snoring over the television.

"As the years went on, Sarah would often go through periods where she would seem peaceful and she would sleep through the night in her own bed. But just when we thought she had moved beyond her problems, the fears and sleep problems would start all over again, lasting weeks or even months.

"Sarah was also deeply connected to the spiritual world, a world she remembered quite clearly. At age five, she would tell us about her life before she came down to earth: 'I am from the angelic realms, and I lived in a big golden castle in the clouds.'

"She remembered selecting the parents she wanted to come to on earth. She described concepts that we'd never taught her, such as God's ability to be in more than one place at the same time, and that God could appear to people in many different forms, choosing the form that was the most comfortable for the individual. She said she missed being able to go anywhere or do anything she wanted just by directing her thoughts and making it happen instantaneously.

"One day, she said to me, 'I love you, Mom, you're the best mom I've ever had.' Then she smiled and said, 'I know what you're thinking. You're thinking you're the only mom I've ever had, but I've had many moms in other lifetimes and you are my favorite.'

"Yet despite Sarah's strong connection to the world of light, she was unable to conquer her fears. The sleeping problems continued through the age of nine, and it appeared to boil down to two main fears. First, she was afraid that when she woke up in the morning, both of us, her parents, would be gone, and she would be left all alone. Secondly, she was afraid that a stranger would sneak into the house in the middle of the night and kidnap her or us. Of course, we assured her that her first fear was silly. We would never leave her in the middle of the night. And as for someone coming into our house in the middle of the night, we reminded her of all the strong locks and safety devices in our home. However, these parental reassurances did nothing to satisfy Sarah's unrest.

"She would only sleep on her back at night because she felt as if she always had to have her eyes toward the door so she could spot anyone who tried to come in. She also insisted that the bathroom door next to her bedroom remain closed because she felt this was where the bad spirits would enter her house. (By this age she was no longer calling them clowns but instead recognized them as being bad spirits. As a toddler, the only word she had for scary things came from a character who had once scared her—a clown.)

"Sarah also complained about hearing voices in her head that said scary things to her and sometimes tried to convince her to do bad things. It was at this point that Sarah's parents finally turned to me for assistance."

"I think the first step for Sarah is a past life regression to determine if any of her fears are based on issues from another time." Her parents agreed and we scheduled Sarah's first regression for the end of January.

In the session, Sarah told us, "I am seeing myself as a young girl. My mom is my aunt from this lifetime and my dad is my closest cousin in this lifetime. My name is Katy. I'm just one and I am very happy. I love my mommy and daddy very much."

I took her forward a year. "It's my second birthday and I'm a little sad because my grandpa died yesterday. My grandma is still alive and is my dad in this current lifetime."

As I took her through the years, everything went along smoothly in her life until the age of seven. In the session, Sarah started to cry, and told us, "I wake up one morning and run into my parent's bedroom, but they're not there. I look all over the house, but they're nowhere to be found."

"What did you do next?" I asked.

"I call my grandma," Sarah said, through her tears. "My grandma comes to pick me up and she calls the police. A full month goes by and I have no idea where my mommy and daddy are."

As she described this part of the story, Sarah's voice was filled with so much pain and sadness that her mother and I knew she was truly reliving a painful experience. She told us that after a month, the police informed her and her grandma that her parent's bodies had been found. They had been stabbed to death and their bodies dumped off. "I never found out why someone took my parents from our house or why they were murdered. I lived with my grandma for the rest of that lifetime, but although she was very good to me, I was never happy again in that life."

I then helped Sarah to release the energies from that lifetime that she had carried over with her into this life. This regression certainly explained a lot. First, it revealed why she had that "unfounded" fear that her parents wouldn't be there when she woke up in the morning. And, why she only felt secure if she could sleep in their room so she could be sure they wouldn't leave her. It also explained her fear that a stranger would enter the house in the middle of the night and kidnap her or her parents.

Sarah's mother added, "I was fascinated to learn that her name had been Katy in that lifetime, because at around the age of three, she became obsessed with that name. She insisted that we call her Katy instead of Sarah, and said that she wanted to change her name permanently. When I told her it was okay to pretend, but we had no intention of changing her name officially, she shut herself into her bedroom and cried for over an hour. It was totally out of character for her to display such strong emotions. She responded with the only solution she had control over—she named all of her dolls Katy."

Her mother continued, "It was also interesting that her aunt and cousin were her parents in that life. In this lifetime, her aunt used to baby sit Sarah once a week, and whenever someone would talk to her aunt, Sarah would become hysterical and scream until the person went away. It was as if she didn't want to share her aunt's attention with anyone else. It all makes sense now that we know how abruptly she lost them in the past life."

Any doubts that Sarah's parents may have about her concocting this story just to please them were dispelled after they listened to the tape I made of the regression. First of all, there is no way she could make up a story that would cause her to feel such strong emotions that she cry intensely as she described what happened. And secondly, so many aspects of that life were intricately connected to details in this life that she never could have thought through all of this on a conscious level and put it into a believable story. Also, if a nine-year-old was inventing a story about a past life, she would probably have made everyone the same gender in the past life as they are in the current life. But, her past grandmother became her current father and her past father became her current female cousin. All of this made it quite clear to me and her parents that this was a genuine past life experience.

Vanishing Veil

We all hoped that this regression would bring an end to Sarah's nocturnal troubles, and while it certainly improved matters, we still weren't done. So she came back for two more regressions.

In the second regression, Sarah reported, "I am the third child in a family of four children. We live on a farm and my family is very poor, but I am happy."

However, we hit trouble in her 11th year. "I am awakened by my older brother. He's telling me that our mom and dad took off in the middle of the night and abandoned us. He'd heard them talking about how we're too much for them to handle and they can't see how they can afford to raise us any longer. They think that if the leave, someone else will take care of us much better than they ever could."

Going forward in time, Sarah told us, "In fact, an aunt and uncle did take us in, but I never saw my mom and dad again."

In the third regression, Sarah explained, "I am a boy named George. My dad is having an affair with another woman. One day, when I am ten, my mother finds out and shoots my father. Then she runs away to avoid getting into trouble and I never see her again."

Both of these past lives continued the theme of parents abandoning their children without warning. No wonder little Sarah carried over her insecure feelings and was afraid to let her parents out of her sight!

After the release work I took Sarah through on these past lives, she was no longer afraid of sleeping in a separate room from her parents. But we still hadn't closed the door on her nocturnal problems. She was still having those "voices" in her head at night which scared her, and she still sensed some lower entities were around her. When I meditated and went in on Sarah, I saw that she had picked up a couple of lost souls in the hospital when she had her adenoids removed seven years earlier, and they were still with her. I recommended a clearing, which we scheduled for mid-February.

In the clearing, Sarah identified the two spirits in her that she had picked up at the hospital. She told us, "One is a teenage boy who died when he was hurt in a motorcycle accident. The other is a young girl who died after a long, serious illness."

Sarah felt them both leave her body. Then, curious, I aimed a question at Sarah's higher self. "Why are these two spirits putting scary thoughts into her head?"

Sarah responded, "It's coming mostly from the teenage boy. He isn't a bad person, just a confused lost soul. He doesn't understand why he can't communicate with anyone on earth anymore and it frustrates him. He's tried to communicate nice thoughts, but gets no reaction from me. But when he communicates scary or bad thoughts, I react. This gives him the satisfaction of knowing he still has an existence and can interact with the earth plane. He was a little sad to let go of my body and go to the light. He said that he had enjoyed living life through me, especially the nice vacations I went on."

Sarah's mother called me a few days later. "Sarah's reaction to the clearing really surprised me. For days afterwards, she talked about how empty she felt inside of her, 'I'm feeling lonely now that they're gone, I don't even know who Sarah is. I'm not sure what thoughts have been mine all these years and what thoughts were theirs.' "

I suggested, "Tell Sarah to continually fill that empty space inside of herself with white light until she adjusts to living her life as a solo act again."

Comments on Sarah

A lot happened to that little girl in such a short time, and it's no wonder that she felt empty. However, after the initial adjustment, which took less than a week, the changes in Sarah were remarkable. She was finally able to go to bed at night without any fears or voices. At the end of that week, her mother went upstairs to check on her because the bathroom door was wide open and she couldn't hear Sarah snoring. Then she noticed that her daughter was lying on her stomach in bed, something she had never done, and, for the first time since she was two, she was breathing soundlessly.

8. Emily

When Emily arrived for the session, she was very tense. So I lightly said, "Relax, and I'll see who you brought with you. The spirits almost always come in the order of importance that they are or were in your life. Now here's one who came instantly, wanting to come in first. I'm seeing a man, he's not very tall. He has a small frame, wears glasses and his hair is or was dark. I'm sometimes not sure what side of the veil they're on. If you recognize the spirit, say a first name, then they actually shake their head 'yes' or 'no' if that is who they are. Do you know this man?"

"Yes, it's Bruce."

"He nodded his head, yes. Who is this?" I asked.

"He's my father."

"He is here so clearly. In fact, he was here even before I closed my eyes and I always ask them not to come until I close my eyes or put them out of focus, because it gets so distracting. Has he been on the other side long?"

"Almost six years."

"I'm picking up that he was a very quiet person. He's asking me to tell you, 'I don't feel that I was able to convey my true feelings to you as much as I'd wished. You were so very special to me.' He has a very warm smile. He's on the right side of the couch, and he just kind of curled up and has his arm around you. You may feel a warmth or a tingling."

Emily nodded and said, "Yes, I do."

"You're going to feel him like that again, when you're not with me. He did that so I could relay to you what that feeling was, but now when you feel it, be sure you mentally say, 'Hi, Dad, thanks for coming.' The more you mentally talk to him, the more you open up your channels and the easier it is for him to come in. And he wants very much to make a connection with you. I feel your Dad had a real nurturing aspect, and that he chose to be one of your main guides when he crossed over. So, he's around you all the time.

"He's showing me having you meditate and my feeling is, Emily, that you are going to have your messages come through very clearly. Once you get into an altered state of consciousness and just ask him a question, you'll hear him. It'll come in thought form and at first you'll think it's your own thoughts. But, his telepathy is very strong, and you'll even know by the wording that it's him. You are going to think, 'Oh, I wouldn't have a thought like that.' Well, that's his thought."

Just then, there was an almost imperceptible creaking noise. "Did you hear that sound like a house settling?" I asked Emily.

She nodded yes.

"That's the spirits' sound. For some reason, it's a sound that's very easy for them to make. So, even if you're talking to someone else, when you hear that sound, mentally acknowledge the fact that you're aware of his presence. Skeptics will say it sounds like a room settling, and that's exactly what it sounds like, but I'm sure you noticed it came from right here in the middle of the room, it wasn't in the walls."

Again, Emily nodded.

I continued, "He's telling me that however you heard about me, he's taking credit for it. He's gone to quite some length to get you to see me because he wants so much to be able to communicate with you. By the way, he's standing behind you now."

As Emily glanced over her shoulder, I went on, "I feel that you came to life this time to be a service person, which is what I consider myself to be. I see you being in metaphysics quite strongly, even to the point where someday you will teach metaphysics. I'm seeing you starting off in a home situation, with small groups and then moving on to some pretty large groups. I'm seeing you in a room like a hotel, a room that has a lot of chairs and people in it. Again,

I don't get timing, but I'm seeing you get involved with some type of a group that maybe meets monthly where people meditate and do some metaphysical types of things. You're going to be such a natural at it. I'm also seeing you do some one-on-one work with people, maybe healing."

"Would I be doing this work with people who are involved with violence?" Emily asked.

"I'm getting a 'yes' on that, which makes sense with what I saw. I saw you doing healings and using metaphysics. It's going to start off just as something to do and grow from there. Even though I feel you're very good at what you are doing now, I feel that some day you'll be away from that, and believe it or not, it's going to be more gratifying than your teaching. You have spirits all around you."

After a pause to let all that information sink in, I said, "Let's see who else is here. I'm seeing a lady, she's about medium height, a little heavy set, her hair is salt and pepper, but more salt than pepper, she either wore it close to her head or pulled back. Do you know who this lady is?"

"Is it Lucy?"

"Yes."

"She's my mother."

"She's on the other side, isn't she?"

"Yes," Emily said, nodding.

"I feel such a sadness with her. Does that make sense?"

"Yes."

"As she matches my frequency, it almost makes me want to cry. She's saying, 'It was all so senseless, but don't worry about it. We've worked through it. It took me longer than Dad. I love you, I'm proud of the way you've handled things. Good comes from many things. This will help to put you on your path.' I feel they both died suddenly. Is that right?"

"Yes."

"She does want you to know that she is okay. She was a very strong lady, wasn't she?"

"Yes."

"I just feel her taking over me and that doesn't normally happen to this extent. She's saying to you, 'You are stronger than you give yourself credit for, and have become much more so since this happened. I'm helping people who have been murdered to adjust to this side—it's confusing when you go so quickly. I'm getting great satisfaction from this. This is how I have chosen to grow and evolve spiritually on this side. We will be doing similar type of work, only on different sides of the veil.' "

"I was kind of curious, who is turning off the lights?"

"Your dad."

"Well, tell him he picks rather inopportune times to shut off the lights."

"How funny, once a father always a father."

Emily smiled.

"He's back sitting beside you and has his arm around you and he's really chuckling about this along with us. Wow, you have the loudest spirits around you! That was your mother. Really, a client may hear one or two but yours are really loud. You've got to be aware of them now. They're really giving you a show. This is really very heavy isn't it?"

Emily nodded.

"I'm getting that both your parents were killed by a brother. Is he your brother?"

"No, my uncle."

"It's your mother's brother. I should have known—she's the one who said, 'Brother'."

"I guess I want to make sure that they understand that Jane, my sister, and I are fine and that we've not adjusted, but we've come to terms with everything, and that we hope that we settled their estate the way they wanted it ..."

"Your mom has tears coming down her face when you're talking."

"... and, that we miss them."

"She's bending over you and saying, 'We miss you, too.' She's placing her cheek against your cheek and you might even feel her. She's very emotional right now."

Sensing that we were coming to the end of the session, I asked, "Do you have any questions?"

"Do you see anything about the man who's in my life right now?" Emily asked.

"What's his first name?"

"Greg."

"Is he kind of big?"

"Yes."

"I'm getting that he has a hard time with commitment. I feel he worships you, and he's very sincere and trustworthy, and very much in love with you. He's had some bad experiences with women though, hasn't he?"

"Yes."

"And you're paying for it. What a shame, because he's never been so in love as he is with you. And yet, because of those past experiences, he's having a terrible time. And, also, unfortunately, it looks like he's built up some real thick walls around himself."

"Yes."

"It's like, 'I'll let you in so far, but don't try to come that last couple of inches.' Actually, he's more vulnerable than he wants anyone to know, including you. This sensitivity, which is one of the things you love about him so much, is one of the things keeping him away from you, too. Does that make sense?"

"Yes."

"He's just put up this wall because, 'I don't want to be hurt again!' "

"He says that metaphysics is funny and silly. But, I'm wondering if he's a lot more interested in it than he says."

"Yes, he really hasn't thought about it that much, but he has a very strong sixth sense, call it what you want—men usually call it a gut feeling or a hunch. I feel he's more scared of it than anything."

"I hope my parents are all right with this relationship."

"Yes, they're telling me that they like him very much. Is Greg getting bored with his job? I'm seeing BORED written in gigantic print."

"That's the understatement of the year."

"He needs to move on. He's so bored that it's ridiculous. He's almost having trouble doing a good job, which he's very capable of doing. He's going to get another job. It's going to be in some type of sales. I feel he's very good at sales."

"Outstanding."

"I'm hearing the current job is not challenging, I want to say to him to keep looking in the paper. I just feel that something is going to come right out from the paper and just hit him and he's going to say, 'Yep, that's for me, thank you very much.' And after five years of being together, I do think that some day you'll get him to the altar."

"That would be nice."

"I'm seeing you go through the ceremony, I don't know why that ceremony scares him to death, but it does."

"He can't even watch it on television."

"Now that's what I call a block!"

"You know, Marge, my Mom was paralyzed on one side because she had polio as a child. When you got into her energy earlier on, you assumed the exact same position she always had when sitting, kind of leaning to one side. And you held your hands just like she did. You even had her facial expressions, voice tone, and vocabulary."

Comments on Emily

How hard to lose both parents at once, especially at the hands of a relative, so I was pleased that Emily physically felt her father's presence, and heard her mother's. That's so comforting!

Having her mom's energy "pop" into mine is very typical. The spirits are so eager to have their loved ones left here on the earth plane to have no doubt that it is them channeling through me. This is similar to possession, except after every reading that

I do, I demand that my clients and his or her spirit friends leave me and my house. Otherwise it would be impossible for me to distinguish my energies from everyone else's, because during a reading, I purposely go into my client's energy.

Emily needs to do a lot of forgiving with her uncle. In the Lord's prayer, it says, "Forgive us our trespasses as we forgive those who trespass against us." This forgiveness is an essential ingredient for growing spiritually.

9. Mindy

Mindy was born in 1945, just at the end of WWII. Laura, her mother, had inadvertently got pregnant in a love affair, as many did just after the war. She was unable to tell her parents, but in the end, she had to tell them since she was a good Catholic girl. It was an extremely painful time for her, and she had to make some very difficult decisions. Her parents were not supportive, so she was faced with giving Mindy up for adoption.

Laura had a best friend, Mary, and she placed Mindy with Mary's parents as foster parents as a way of avoiding giving her daughter up completely. Laura visited her, and even Laura's parents visited occasionally. When Mindy was a year old, Laura signed her over for adoption to Mary's parents because she'd met a young man and wanted to start a family, but was terrified of telling him that she'd had an illegitimate child. Everyone was happy, and even her priest told her not to look back.

Laura and Mary never saw each other again. Mary never let Laura know about Mindy's progress, and Laura lost touch with her daughter.

Mindy grew up in a dysfunctional family. She had three different fathers, one an abusive alcoholic, and a very unhappy adoptive mother. Mindy believes that her upbringing gave her strength of character and prompted her to begin a process of self-healing in her mid-thirties.

Wanting to know who she was and where she came from, Mindy began searching for her birth mother, Laura, and found her in 1986.

They took a year to actually meet because Laura was quite fearful of her husband and children finding out about her past.

Laura had had two daughters, and then two sons. When Mindy and Laura met in 1987, Laura' husband was ill, and she was under a lot of strain, topped by the problem of having to confess to her husband that she'd never confided in him about Mindy. She was afraid that her husband and children would think terrible thoughts of her, that she was a whore, that she was some kind of an awful person because she'd had an illegitimate child. Over the years, Laura had worried herself into heart disease. She'd had several angioplasties and was looking at coronary bypasses.

Mindy came to see me in 1991 at the suggestion of a friend. As soon as she walked in, a male being showed up from the spirit world.

"Your father is here; your birth father. His Higher Self is telling you, through me, 'You chose me as your biological father even though we had only been connected in one other life. You came into this world and the adoptive process to learn the lessons you needed to learn.'"

"What about my birth mother, Laura?" Mindy asked.

"She's right here, Mindy," I said. "I know it's her from the description you gave me. She's saying she wants to meet your daughters very much. Even though they're grown, (20 and 23, I later found out), she's saying she doesn't have the right to interfere in your life."

Just then, I felt a severe pain in my chest. When I tried to rub the pain away, Mindy said, "My mother has some heart problems."

I knew that the problem stemmed from the heartache she had borne for 45 years. After a few more family details were exchanged, the session ended.

Mindy came back for another session about six months later, and I performed a regression on her to do a "forgive and release" around her adopted mother, Mary. I put her in a bubble, and Mindy let her go, cutting the cord connecting the two of them. Then we did some work with Laura, her birth mother, which Mindy found to be cathartic and very healing.

Mindy continued to study with me and learned to meditate. She also brought her daughters down, and lo and behold, Laura popped up in their readings to reiterate that she wants to meet them but feels she has no right to interfere in their lives. She said through me, "I'm 'stuck,' really stuck."

Although Laura is Mindy's mother, Mindy doesn't have any feelings about her as a mother, nor does Laura have any feelings towards Mindy as a daughter because of the years they spent apart. But as people, they're connected, and they wanted to put some of their feelings to rest, such as Laura's guilt and Mindy's anger, rejection, and abandonment common with many adoptees.

Mindy wrote to her mother suggesting this but got no reply, so she called. Laura explained, "I can't go through with it because I just can't tell my children."

Mindy replied, "This isn't about your children. It's about you and me, and they don't have to know."

Of course, Mindy was curious about her siblings because Laura had told her that she looked like them, even though they had a different father. Mindy emphasized again, "This is about us."

Still Laura hesitated, so Mindy did another meditation and saw very, very clearly that she should call her half-brother, Tom, who was a TV network producer. Over lunch, Mindy asked, "Tom, help me with Laura. I really want her to meet my children and grandchildren."

Tom replied, "You know, this is really much bigger than just Laura. Everyone should know."

Tom took it upon himself to tell all the sisters and the other brother, and suddenly Mindy got a whole new family that welcomed her with open arms. They perfectly understood the decision Laura had made in 1945, and were actually angry at her for not telling them back in 1986 when Mindy first contacted her.

On December 12, 1992, Laura called Mindy (Mindy's 47th birthday) and thanked her. She said, "My heart is lighter and I feel so much better now that my children know and have accepted it. I am so happy."

Laura's husband had passed away in 1990, and she has started on her own healing path. Mindy's path opened up Laura's path, who is in the process of forgiving herself and dealing with the fact that she never told her husband. She's also talking it out with her children. They are a very close family and they are all helping Laura with that. Their loving acceptance has helped a great deal. Mindy and Laura genuinely like one another and see each other every other week for lunch.

Having healed their relationship, they would both like to see Mary who brought Mindy up. Mary stopped speaking to Mindy when she began to look for her birth mother. Mindy feels the need to deal with that and achieve closure. Someday, she hopes to summon up the courage to do that.

Laura is now approaching the end of her life and found that getting the story out in the open proved to be very healing. She had actually been writing her memoirs on Tom's computer, and she was going to seal them in an envelope in a safe deposit box to be read when she passed on. However, Mindy wouldn't let her do that, sensing all the good that would come out of open disclosure—new brothers and sisters, new feelings, a sense of completeness. Mindy is now enjoying Laura and all of her children and grandchildren. Laura's face now glows with light, and she feels so much better that it brings Mindy to tears.

Mindy often calls me and thanks me for having gotten her started not only in her own work through my seminars, but for showing her how to channel healing energy.

I once asked Mindy, "Did Laura resent you going to her son?"

"Yes, in a way she did. I'll tell you the story. I called and left him a message at the TV studio. He's a producer and he's done documentaries on adoption before."

"That's interesting. You know, Mindy, there's no such thing as a coincidence."

"Tom called me back, and he didn't know who I was. He

thought I was looking for a job. I didn't want to tell him the story on the phone; I wanted to get him to lunch and tell him then. He thought I was some kind of a crackpot, either looking for work, or whatever, because I told him I had a story to tell him. I didn't mention adoption.

"Later that night, Tom told Laura, 'Boy, mom I got the craziest phone call this afternoon from some woman called Mindy.' Well, that started my mother thinking and she decided to spill the beans to Tom. 'Mindy is my daughter from before I married your father.'

"Tom fell out of his chair when she told him the story. He immediately called me and we agreed to meet the next day. He was suspicious about what it was that I wanted from them. Playing the protective elder son, he refused to set up a one-on-one meeting between his mom and me. Instead, he announced, 'I'm going to tell everyone so that we can all rally around and support her.'

"It took Laura a while to trust me because I was a disruption in her life. She did resent that. But now when we go to lunch, she'll put her arm in mine and walk along, and give me a hug, or whatever. Last week at lunch, she looked at me and said, 'You know, I really like you, I don't feel about you like I would one of my other daughters, but I like you.' "

Comments on Mindy

My seminars got Mindy started on a path of knowing herself on a much deeper level, and empowered her to make healthy choices in her life, to heal her relationships, and to be a stronger more fulfilled person. Her guides are starting to come to her, and she's opened a dialogue with them. She now feels like she has help and that she's getting closer to her life purpose.

When you're around negative people, or people full of fear, as Laura was when Mindy resurfaced in her life, open up your heart. Let them experience your love. Everything that someone does is either love or a call for love.

See obstacles as opportunities or an adventure. Don't become a victim. Mindy opened up to her spirituality because of her search for her biological mom. Her spiritual adventure has totally changed her life in an extremely positive way.

We have to be willing to give up our attachment to a particular outcome in a given situation. Laura and Mindy will never have the mother-daughter relationship that Mindy had been searching for, but Mindy went with the flow of the situation and now has new friends and family.

As you look back on your life and review your past relationships (even those you are still letting go of), see how they served you. What you have now would not be possible without those experiences. The more you hate something, the more bound you are to it, and the more you love it, the freer you are. So as you love your past, you free yourself from it.

10. Cheryl

Cheryl first came to see me about three years after her husband, Walt, died in an industrial accident. I had been recommended by her mother (who had worked with me in the toy business). Cheryl only half believed in metaphysics at the time and came to me as a skeptic.

A man showed up immediately and I described him and some of his mannerisms.

"That's Walt to a tee," she shouted. "Physical appearance is one thing, but you even captured his personality, the traits that were really him. That's all the proof I need. It's him all right. We were married almost a year and then he was killed in an industrial accident at work. It was sudden and totally unexpected."

"He wants me to tell you that he's okay and not to worry about him."

"So, what is he doing over there?" Cheryl asked.

"He tells me that he's working with children who have just passed over."

"It makes me feel better to know that he has a real purpose and that he's contributing at a much higher level than he could have if he stayed here," Cheryl admitted.

"Was he real good with children while he was alive?"

"Yes, he had a great rapport with children. It makes me feel better that he's doing something he was good at and that he is really contributing. Everyone says, 'There's a bigger reason for this,' or, 'There has to be a higher purpose,' but to really have it illustrated is very healing."

I told Cheryl, "I can feel his love and concern for you. He's telling me to tell you that even though he can't be with you the way it was before, you could keep helping each other in different ways. If you're up to it, he wants to show you how you can be more aware of his presence. Listen for the 'clicking' noise that he makes to get your attention."

Cheryl became such a believer that she began to attend my seminars. She opened up to the energy of a group, especially a group that comes together for a single purpose, and where everyone has pretty much the same beliefs. She learned to meditate and found how it changed her life. She was fascinated to learn the incredible power of the human mind and how easy it is to send thoughts and energy.

In another session, I did some automatic writing for her from Walt. He wrote about ten short lines. "That's Walt," she said. "No doubt about it. That's him. True to his fashion, he starts out with a compliment to you. And he mentions your pool. He likes your pool. He was a swimmer. Then there's some messages of love. He's written something to my Mom. He calls her 'Ma,' which is what he always called her. He's also written a message to his best friend who's going through some tough times. There's absolutely no doubt in my mind that it's Walt giving us messages through your hand because the messages are so concrete. It's really healing and assuring. I feel so much better. Thank you."

Cheryl returned home to Chicago where she shared an apartment with her best friend, Deb. Deb was fairly open to spirituality, but Cheryl's experiences really scared her a lot, especially when Cheryl returned all excited and told her everything. Deb admitted, "I would be so scared if I felt a presence, or if I thought there was a spirit in the room. I'd rather have something that was okay, something that I wasn't scared about."

As they walked into the living room together, a music box suddenly started playing. Deb's eyes got so big, and she said, "It's him, isn't it?"

"What do you think?" Cheryl asked.

A panicked Deb said, "I know it is."

In fact, they both knew it was Walt. The music box had never played by itself before. After a few more experiences, Deb got less and less scared.

Cheryl kept reminding her, "Well, you weren't scared of him when he was alive, and he's not going to come and hurt you or anything."

I also gave Cheryl a past life regression while I was giving a seminar and doing readings and regressions in Chicago. That also was a real healing experience for her: "We went back into another life when I was married to Walt. At the end of that lifetime, I allowed myself to die of a broken heart over the loss of my children and grandchildren. I felt very strongly that I was abandoning him. I think that really helped me to understand this lifetime and my feelings of abandonment when he died. It made me realize fully that things don't just happen randomly, and that there's a reason for his death. I'm learning from this experience. It makes it easier to live through if you at least know that you are learning from it. It's like, 'I chose this so I could learn this lesson.' It's not just a random event in the universe."

Cheryl sent another friend, Shirley, to me and I gave her a past-life regression. She was deeply distraught over not being able to have children. She later told me, "I went back and found that in more than one lifetime that I'd abandoned my children, and that

I'd decided in this lifetime that I had to work through that before I would be able to have my own children again."

After much inner work and self-forgiveness, at age 42, she was finally surprised to find she was pregnant after she and her husband had exhausted all medical possibilities. Soon after her son was born, she told me, "You know, I really feel like that regression was a turning point in my life. When I went back, I discovered that I'd had some negative experiences with children before, and that in my subconscious mind, I held so much guilt that I was afraid to have my own children again. I really feel that I worked through that, and once I did, I soon got pregnant."

Comments on Cheryl and Shirley

The importance of regression is a recurring theme. In this case, Shirley needed to forgive herself for her actions towards children in a previous life. What a marvelous outcome for her! As always, the most important person to forgive is yourself, either for what you did or for wanting or needing that experience.

11. Mary

Mary and her husband had moved into a quaint home in an older part of the city. After only a short time, out of their peripheral vision, they began to notice a white, wispy form moving about. It seemed to always originate from one bedroom, and try as they might, they could not ignore it. Even their friends started to notice it without being prompted. That's when they called me and asked me to come over and see what I could pick up psychically.

I put myself into an altered state of consciousness and described their "ghost."

"I'm seeing a male. He is average-to-short in height, a little overweight, short brown hair, and he looks to be in his twenties. He was an only child, born to an older couple. His parents were extremely over-protective of him. For years, he'd wanted a motorcycle but was held back from getting one by his parents. But, eventually they relented and he bought a gorgeous, large motorcycle. He was so proud of this possession that he actually kept it in the house, in his bedroom to be precise, the same room you keep seeing a "ghost" emerge from. Soon after he got it, he had a fatal accident. His parents never recovered emotionally from his death. Their son, distraught over the grief he caused his parents, remains on the earth plane, and in particular the room in the house where he was brought up. His parents crossed over soon after his accident. It feels like they died of broken hearts."

I talked to him and told him, "Go to the light."

That worked because Mary said that they didn't see him after that. Full of curiosity, Mary and her husband began to question the neighborhood looking for someone who had lived there long enough to know this family. They did, and learned that everything I saw psychically was exactly what had happened, even down to the appearance of the son.

A year or so later, Mary and her husband moved into a much newer home and had their first baby. Jennifer would wake up nightly and when they tiptoed into her room, they would find her looking into thin air and smiling. They also heard strange clicking noises, a common "spirit sound." Out of desperation to get a full night's sleep, they asked if I would once more go over to see what or who was keeping their baby up most of the night.

On entering their home, I immediately saw an older lady. I described her and Mary said, "That's my grandma. She's on the other side and always did love children."

"Well, that's who's playing with Jennifer every night. You can mentally or out loud converse with Grandma and simply tell her that you're happy she is playing with your baby, but to please come and play with her during the day."

Mary did just that, and Grandma willingly obliged. End of sleepless nights!

Comments on Mary

The young man with his motorcycle needed to be prodded to finally go into the light and continue on his spiritual path. It often happens that someone who has crossed over doesn't immediately go to the light. The spirit isn't interested in merging with someone else's energy, but simply stays in a physical place where he or she had been happy and content, or feels the need to assuage guilt towards a family member(s), even when the family doesn't live there anymore.

12. Karen

Karen came to see me at the suggestion of a total stranger she met on an airplane while going over to Hawaii. She struck up a conversation with this woman and just seemed to hit it off. When she confided in Janine, her new friend, that her only son had taken his life a year earlier, Janine said, "I'm a crisis counselor and I suggest that you meet someone I've heard of who is very much into metaphysics and might be able to help you."

This all sounded totally foreign to Karen at the time, and kind of spooky, so she put it out of her mind. Karen and her husband had a wonderful time on their trip with the woman and her husband and kept in touch. Each time they met, Janine brought up my name and suggested Karen get in touch with me. Karen still didn't take the bait until Janine told her where I lived. It turned out that I was a neighbor of Karen's son's best friend. Also, I lived just three minutes from Karen's home. That coincidence definitely got her attention.

Before we go any further, let me back up to the day before Karen's son, Ron, took his life. She met him at school (he was a freshman in college at Santa Cruz, California), and they went out to lunch, as they periodically did. After lunch, Ron insisted that they go to a specific beach. It was quite a long drive and Karen said that she wasn't sure she wanted to go.

Ron insisted, saying, "Let's go, I'd like you to see it."

They walked on the beach and enjoyed a long conversation. Ron was quite idealistic about how things should be, and he expressed some major concerns about their family life and the way things were in general, such as people's attitudes. It wasn't a real upbeat conversation from Karen's perspective, but it wasn't the type of thing that she took as a dangerous sign of any problems or anything. Before they parted, she hugged him and told him how much she loved him and how proud she was of him. Looking back on it now, she is so glad that she had that opportunity.

The next day, Karen and her husband learned that a fisherman had found Ron's body on the same beach he'd taken her to.

When Karen came to me, I knew none of this. I saw a young man and described him to Karen. She gasped at the accurate picture, and confirmed that it was Ron.

"I'm seeing him on a beach," I said.

"Would you ask him how he felt about his memorial service?" Karen asked.

"He's telling me that he was at the service in Santa Cruz and was very touched by it, especially by what you said."

Karen later told me that her delivering the eulogy was totally out of character for her. She'd never spoken to a crowd in her life before, but she felt that there were things that needed to be said to the group of college kids. She said the help she got from Ron really made things a lot smoother, otherwise she could never have done it under any other circumstances.

"Ron is telling me that most of his unhappiness was caused by his father who is a heavy drinker and verbally very abusive. He is very unhappy that you are still in that situation. He is trying from the other side to encourage you to leave his dad and stresses that he would be with you and help you and give you the strength."

Karen later told me that this inside family information was a real confirmation to her that it was indeed Ron. In fact, after their last walk, Ron's last words to her were, "Do whatever it takes to make yourself happy."

It took Karen three years to leave her husband, and her biggest regret is that she didn't do it when Ron was alive. Maybe he'd still be alive! With this loss of her beloved son, she was frantically trying to reach him since the only thing she could think of was Ron's well-being. I was honored to be able to tell her that he was safe, gathering strength, and happy.

After this communication, Karen now has no fear of death and knows that she can reach through the veil and contact people on the other side. She also learned that we constantly get guidance and love from people who have crossed over. Whenever she is "down" or there is a problem, Ron is always there to comfort her and lend his strength. She can feel his presence physically, as something that washes over her and takes the sadness away.

"It's the next best thing to having him with me physically. It offers me hope and takes away my fear," she said. "There's no longer a finality to death. Things can still be recaptured. These people aren't lost, they are in fact still with us."

Also, in the reading, Ron told me, "After gathering my strength, I'm going to greet teen suicides as they cross over. And in helping others to adjust, I'm gathering strength for myself. I really enjoy this type of work, as I did on earth."

This surprised Karen, since I had no way of knowing that Ron was a peer counselor and was trained to work with teenagers, counseling them against suicide, drugs, and addictions. He was very good at helping everyone else.

In a later reading, Ron came through with a touching message for his mother. "First, I'd like people to know that those of us who take our own lives are not necessarily weak, and that on the level of our higher selves, we know that we will accomplish more on the other side. There's so much derogatory judgment when someone commits suicide and, yes, it's probably slowed up my progress a little, but I am well and actively working at my spiritual evolution. On earth, I, like many others, became caught up in the everyday world, even though I tried very hard to put my priorities in the right place and help as many people as I could.

"I was like a sponge and picked up on other people's energies. I took them in and then had trouble realizing where my energies stopped and theirs began. I'm learning a lot through you, Mom, now that you're on your spiritual pathway, and it's helping me. As you know, I wasn't aware of all of this metaphysics on the earth plane. You *can* make things happen on earth, Mom, as you can make things happen here, and that is what I realized through you and your studies.

"As for poor Dad, I'm really in a place now where I can feel sorry for him. He's so far off his path that I don't see him returning to it in this lifetime. I can only pray for him now. But it's easier to see his problems and human frailties from this vantage point than it was as his son on the earth plane. So, believe me, Mom, we'll have no problems when he crosses over. I've been able to forgive him completely. Maybe in some respects, he did me a favor as I'm accomplishing so much here. The stronger I get, the easier it is for me to come through to you.

"I'm working on your trust, Mom, because you're getting more from me than you'll admit to yourself. Just keep meditating. The stronger I get, the more accurately I can see into the future for you. Your growth comes from your own choices. You've made some right choices lately and you've put yourself on a completely different path. I'm glad."

Karen replied, "So many people who have gone through a similar type of situation take a different path, rather than a metaphysical one. I'm sure that metaphysics is the only path that would have offered me any sort of comfort whatsoever. The academic approach isn't at all consoling to me. The metaphysical aspect of life after death, and being able to make some kind of contact and be reassured that you'll be able to spend some time together is very healing for me."

Comments on Karen

Isn't it interesting that Karen gets on an airplane to Hawaii, distraught over her only child taking his life, and sits next to a crisis counselor? Coincidence? No!

The crisis counselor has heard about me! I share a driveway with one of Ron's best friends! I live three minutes from Karen's house! Coincidence? No!

In Ron's case, he is a very highly evolved soul who chose a difficult life, feeling he could use the lessons he would learn as stepping stones to his spiritual growth, and not stumbling blocks. We do pick our parents, even though it's hard to believe sometimes. He knew his dad would have a drinking problem but he felt he could grow from the lessons he'd learn from this situation. Ron did grow, as you read. While alive, he worked with troubled teenagers even though he himself had many troubles of his own to deal with. He was an extremely sensitive being who took others problems on as his own.

When there's a young death, there is soul growth for the whole family.

As a footnote, Ron's dad crossed over with a heart attack a few years after Ron's crossing.

13. Cathy

Cathy was diagnosed with breast cancer and scheduled to have a mastectomy in two weeks. She came to me for a regression so that I could take her back to cause, and to help her to forgive and release things from her past, hoping that in so doing, it would alleviate some of her physical problem, or at least stop it from spreading.

Cathy's mother had found out she had breast cancer in October of her 51st year, and Cathy, too, found that she had breast cancer in October when she was 51. I realized how serious this was because her mother had died just six months later in the following April. Cathy was also worried about a strong feeling she had that her husband would die in April even though he wasn't sick.

Another puzzle piece: Cathy was 20 years old when her mother died, and her mother's friends always remarked about how much Cathy reminded them of her mother in the way she expressed herself verbally and through her gestures.

Once in the session, I realized that Cathy's mother had merged with her at the time of her death and took the blueprint of her body into Cathy. Hence the cancer. We decided to do a clearing rather than a regression.

During the clearing, besides feeling the mother leave, three others also left: an old high school boyfriend who died when he was 21, an artist friend who died 10 years ago, and the lady from LA who used to do Cathy's astrology and psychic readings. I joked with Cathy, "You're like a big sponge to many entities."

After the session, Cathy said, "I'm really angry with my mother for causing me all this trouble. Besides the mastectomy, which in itself is bad enough, I'm also scheduled for two reconstructive surgeries. But at least with my mother out of my body, I already feel very different. And I now realize that my mother has been intimidating me sexually all my life."

"For protection, Cathy, mentally put up a clear glass screen around yourself for a few days because I am seeing your mother trying to get back into you."

It was a couple of weeks before she felt comfortable enough to drop the shielding.

"In retrospect," Cathy later told me, "I realize the importance of forgiveness because of all the opportunities in my life to forgive people, but why did I have to get cancer to do it! Why couldn't I have done it the easy way?" she asked. "But, on the other hand, I can see that it had to be really drastic to make me realize what I needed to do in my life—to forgive and release people and events in my past."

Comments on Cathy

Cathy was hesitant at first to banish her mother from her body because she had become very used to feeling her presence, not realizing the damage she was doing. But I managed to convince her that it was best for both of them to help her mother to go to the light. "You must reclaim your body, and reclaim your life." To her credit, she did.

Over the years, many cancer clients have said to me, "This is the best thing that ever happened to me. A disease such as cancer can be a wake-up call."

When we bury resentments, angers and hurts, and don't deal with them, they must find their own way out. These negatives often manifest themselves in the form of a physical illness. Very often, we get a terminal disease because we've been holding things inside us and not expressing ourselves. Often it's resentment from childhood. We need to go back and deal with those childhood issues. We need to go back and forgive and release. We don't need to condone. Have your higher self forgive their higher self. Whether it cures you or not is up to your soul, but it makes your transition much smoother. You're in a happier state.

Cathy's case is another case of a relative crossing over and yet not wanting to leave the astral plane. Reluctant to go, her mother merged her energies with Cathy's. No wonder her mother's friends saw her mother in Cathy. Edgar Cayce pointed out that spirit possession can be a cause of disease because the possessing entities bring their blueprints with them.

As a footnote, it has been six years since that session and Cathy's cancer has completely disappeared.

14. Patti

Patti had brought a photo of her 16-year-old son. I looked at his picture and saw the word "resentment" written across it in gigantic print. When I mentioned this, Patti started to cry. She told me, "If I had to describe in one word how my son feels about me, that's exactly the word I'd use. But I didn't understand why."

I saw why. "In a past life, you were engaged to be married, but you started to have an affair with someone else—your second husband in this life. You broke off the engagement, and when your fiancé found out about the affair, he climbed through the window of your remote log cabin in the middle of the night strangled you to death."

I also relayed the information, "For karmic reasons, you two needed to come back together this time. He chose to come in as your son."

At that, Patti gasped and said, "During my pregnancy, I frequently had nightmares of being strangled. The nightmares stopped when he was born."

"Your son felt betrayed, abandoned and unloved by you in that past life and he brought those emotions forth into this life. Soon after conceiving your son, you, being very sensitive, you started picking up his energy which still held his anger and the memory of strangling you. In this life, he feels you don't love him. He feels in competition with your current husband, who happens to be the one you ran off with in the past life. So there's a three-way karmic tie between you all. He also feels resentment towards your husband for taking his mother's love away from him once again. He's dealing with a double-edged sword. He feels resentful from that past life because you dumped him for someone else, yet he owes you because he snuffed your life from you when you were in your prime."

Comments on Patti

No one can give information to someone else about a past life that doesn't ring a bell somewhere in his or her subconscious mind. This happened with Patti when I mentioned she was strangled. Again, the puzzle pieces fit together perfectly. It doesn't always solve the problem, but it sure helps us to understand where these feelings are coming from. It helps us to get a life and move on. Patti needs to forgive herself and her son from that past life.

Patti's son hasn't been able to handle or understand his feelings of resentment and anger towards his mom. His way of dealing with all his turbulent feelings was to turn to substance abuse at a very young age.

In a situation like this, we need to focus on what we like about a person, or ourselves, and what we don't like will either not matter as much to you or it will dissipate. Remember, thought is energy, and if we focus on what we don't like about a person, we make it larger. Pay attention to what is right and good in people rather than what they are doing wrong. Also, use inspirational, uplifting words when either thinking or talking about them. Words have energy.

In a karmic relationship, don't let this other person bother you or drain you emotionally. Bless him or her and counteract the whole situation with positive thoughts and sending healing energies. As you do this, the other person will automatically change.

One of the fastest and most effective ways to change anything is to work with the subconscious, putting in new ideas and releasing old ones. Mentally talk to someone who doesn't listen to you. Visualize the other person's face in your mind and talk to him or her mentally, saying everything you've always wanted to say to them. Start by saying, "You are open and receptive to receive what I have to say." Then mentally think positive, loving thoughts into their mind, like, "Mom loves you," and, "Love yourself." If you continue to do this faithfully, it will soon become easier to relate to them verbally.

Also, when people sleep, they're in the theta state, and in deep sleep, they're in the delta level of consciousness. In this state, their subconscious mind is wide open and accepts everything. However, helping others often takes away their power. If you give them a crutch, they may never learn to stand on their own two feet. The practice of "tough love" helps your loved ones to help themselves, so they retain their power and increase their self-esteem.

It's usually better to teach people to fish rather than giving them fish. Often, the most loving thing you can do for people is to stand by while they learn their lessons. If you come in and act as their savior, you may thwart the growth they were getting out of a situation. They will then have to create it all over again. You can, however, assist them from the sidelines by focusing light on them.

15. Sabrina

When Sabrina came to see me, I immediately saw her Grandma who had lived with her and her family all of Sabrina's life. She had just crossed over to the other side, and had a message for Sabrina.

Through me, she said, "Do not to feel guilty. It's okay."

I asked Sabrina if that made sense to her.

"Yes, it does. She'd been very sick and in a rest home the last few years of her life. Going there really depressed me, especially how she looked at the end, so I almost never went to visit her. It makes me feel better to hear that she understood."

She's telling me to tell you to go to the doctor. You need medication."

Sabrina later told me, "I went to the doctor the next day. He told me I had a bad case of bronchitis and that it was good I went in when I did."

The next time I heard from Sabrina was shortly after she'd bought a mobile home. Every night, she was being awakened by loud banging noises on the walls, and she was scared and couldn't sleep. I went over to see "who was there."

I immediately saw an older man and described him to Sabrina.

"That sounds like my grandfather. He crossed over just before I was born, so I never met him."

"Well, he's telling me that he's here to protect you and that he is one of your main spirit guides. He knows that this is a difficult time in your life since it's your first time away from your family. In the future, when you hear that noise, simply say, 'Hi, grandpa, thanks for protecting me.' And, if the sounds bother you, just ask him not be so noisy. Of course, he'll comply."

Sabrina's grandpa left, and was replaced with a new image. "I'm seeing you having the time of your life on a cruise ship," I told her.

"Wow, I'd never even thought about that. I'm looking forward to it already!"

Later, Sabrina told me she welcomed the company of her grandpa, knowing that he was protecting her, but that she was also in complete control.

Comments on Sabrina

It was very healing for Sabrina to hear from her grandmother that it was okay that she didn't visit her much at the end of her life. We often carry around a lot of guilt after loved ones cross over. Remember the most important person for you to ever forgive is yourself.

Know also that we always have control over the spirits. Anytime you feel or hear a spirit in your space and it either annoys or frightens you, firmly tell it to go to the light, and it will. If you don't mind it being around, at least lay down some ground rules for it to follow. The only time this doesn't work is when you're possessed. Then they literally become one with you, merging their energies with yours, so a little more coaxing is necessary, as in a clearing.

By the way, Sabrina soon found herself on a cruise and enjoyed it so much that she signed up for another one almost immediately.

16. Joanne

When I described the first spirit that showed up in Joanne's reading, she said, "That's my grandmother on my mother's side. I'm surprised she came first since you said that they usually appear in the order of importance in my life. She was definitely in my life when I was younger, but she died when I was 10. I haven't thought of her for years."

"Well, she's one of your spirit guides and she has such a strong presence with you."

"I expected my Mom to be the primary guide for me," Joanne said, puzzled. "Now, I'm going to have to start looking at what part my grandmother played in my life. At this point, I don't consciously remember her."

"I think your Mom's here, too," I said and described the other woman standing before me.

"That's very accurate," Joanne said.

"I'm feeling very, very sad," I said. "I just want to cry. Your Mom has become one with me and is crying through me."

Joanne answered, "I wonder why. When my Mom died, I thought she was a real fun-loving person. So why does nothing but sadness seem to be coming through?"

"There's a man here now. He feels like your father. He's crossed over and is carrying a real heavy load of guilt. He was a real angry person while on earth and he's carried a lot of problems with him throughout his life. These problems started in his early childhood."

Then I described a younger man, one who had not yet crossed over.

"That's Victor, my husband."

"I'm seeing that he's having a hard time. He is thinking of suicide. Does that make any sense to you?"

"Yes, it does," she admitted quietly.

Later, Joanne confided in me, "Lately, I've been in a state of denial about a lot of things in my life and haven't been paying much attention to Victor. We're both doing our own thing, but the reading has made me tune into Victor really fast. I hadn't realized how hard this had been on him. My way of handling problems and other people is to keep myself as busy as possible and deny my feelings. The reading played a real key part in helping my relationship with Victor, especially making me realize that I needed to be there more for him."

Next, we came to the main reason Joanne came to me for the reading.

"Susan, my sister, told me that our father had sexually abused her. She realized this through hypnosis and therapy years after he died. It was real hard on me because he was someone I idolized. I was going through denial and anger, not wanting to believe my sister and also feeling that I'd lived a complete lie. And also my Mom, who died recently, had just told me something about my father that I was having a real hard time dealing with. For some reason, Mom felt a need to tell me that Dad wasn't the saint I thought he was, and that he had gone out and had affairs on her their whole marriage. So I grew up thinking that I'd been brought up in a Donna Reed household and all of a sudden, everyone's dead, I'm an adult, and I realize my life wasn't like I had thought it was. Then I started thinking that I wanted to help Susan. I wanted to believe her because I know that if someone says that happened to them, then you have to believe them. But I'm angry with her and my Dad."

"Why don't you come to a class?" I suggested. "There's a new series starting next week."

The first evening of the class, I taught the group how to get into an altered state of consciousness so they could experiment with meditating. Joanne immediately got upset and began to cry because she felt her Dad's presence so strongly and was afraid of encountering him. I saw him standing behind her at that time and confirmed her feelings.

When we did the automatic writing the next day, Joanne was still trying to figure out something about Susan and her relationship with herself and their father. When Susan had originally told her that he'd sexually abused her, Joanne started thinking that both Susan and she had always had problems. Susan had always given Joanne the feeling that Joanne had disappointed her. She was always the disapproving older sister.

Joanne said, "When Susan told me about my Dad, I started thinking, 'Could I possibly have seen something way back then?' So, when I went into the automatic handwriting, I asked to meet up with my mother. And, my question was, 'What is it about my past that always makes me feel like I've let Susan down?'

"After I got into an altered state of consciousness, my first impression was 'explosion,' like a gun shot, and I got lots of feelings. I got two people struggling over me, trying to tell me their side of the story. What I drew, via automatic handwriting, was somebody with a gun, pointing it at a figure. Then, I went on to write, it felt like a real shaky hand was writing through me, and I felt it was my Mom quickly and hurriedly trying to tell me something. I had real strong feelings then of my Dad trying to interfere. I started to cry."

I saw Joanne's Dad, and saw his spirit merge with her body. I saw that he was still earthbound and enjoying life through her. My daughter, Laura, who was sitting beside me at the seminar, saw this happening also. I watched as Joanne's facial expression changed and she got really rigid.

"As I drew the scene with the gun, I felt waves of emotion, as though a struggle was going on inside me as mother and father tried to tell me their sides of the story. None of this made sense to me, and I couldn't figure out what all this had to with my sister, Susan. I felt that my Dad was trying to interfere while I was trying to talk to my Mom about it."

Then I took the group on an astral flight. This is what Joanne experienced:

"That trip you took us on was real good. I met up with my mother and she took me back and helped me have some good memories of childhood. We relived some of our camping trips when I was a child. It was really enjoyable and relaxing. I was amazed at how much detail I got. It's so great to be able to relive my childhood, just Mom and me. We both deliberately kept my Dad out. We were re-experiencing just what she and I had done, without my Dad. I saw even little things, like picking berries. I've always had a hard time remembering my childhood, so this experience was extra special."

Joanne later told me about the first time she attempted to do meditation by herself to get some answers.

"I was sitting on the floor in my toddler's room waiting for her to go to sleep for the night. I asked Mom, 'What else is there that I should know?' Immediately, I saw a faucet with running water and heard, 'Question your brother's death.'

"I'll explain about my brother. Michael died when I was three years old. All I know or remember about him was that he died, and I don't remember any details. I can't even put a face on him. I've never even seen a picture of him. I'd never really thought anything abnormal about his death. We were told he'd died when he was 18 months old of encephalitis and that it was a quick death. Throughout childhood, however, I remember thinking it was a little strange that we were forbidden to ever ask about him. We were simply told that he died, and that was the end of the matter.

"When I was pregnant with Katie, my daughter, I did start thinking about him. During my pregnancy, I visited three of my sisters in New York. I was thinking about being a mother and about my Mom. Suddenly, I thought, 'Gosh, she lost a child when I was three years old.' I started asking innocent questions like how Mom handled Michael's death. My sisters didn't give me any answers. In fact, my oldest sister said, 'I just can't handle talking about it.'

"I thought maybe it was because our Mom had just died and that they didn't want to talk about our Mom, period. This was the only time I questioned it, but I was also thinking at the same time that this must have had an effect on me. So on the Friday night before my regression, I got that strange, off-the-wall message from my Mom: 'Question your brother's death.' "

Joanne came to her regression the next day with the primary intent of seeing whether she had been sexually abused by her Dad, even though she didn't feel in her heart that she had been. Of course, I knew nothing about Michael and what she had gotten the night before. I regressed her to before this current incarnation, and asked her why she was choosing this family to come to.

She said, "So that I would not be loved."

That made no sense to either of us. I saw psychically that she was an older soul and that she had felt she could handle learning to love even though not feeling loved. I then took her to her birth in this life, seeing the faces of her mother and father. We both sensed really good vibrations and a lot of love there. Then I progressed her to her first birthday. Still really good feelings.

"It's around my second birthday, and my brother has just been born. I am experiencing some feelings of jealousy and resentment towards my Mom and Dad because they're giving my brother so much attention. Now it's my third birthday, and I can hear my Mom saying, 'It's bath time.' "

"Who's there with you?" I asked.

In a toddler's voice, Joanne answered, "My Mommy and my brother are here!"

Suddenly, Joanne started screaming and pushing back as though something terrible was happening in front of her. She shouted, "I'm not doing it! I didn't do it! I didn't do it! I didn't do it!"

I asked, "What do you see?"

"I'm at the end of the bath tub and I have this really strong feeling to get as far away from it as possible. 'He's under the water, he's under the water.' "

"Who's under the water?" I asked.

"My brother, he's under the water! Mommy, he's under the water. Get him out!"

By this time, Joanne was really panicking. "Why is he under the water? Where is your Mom? Is your Mom there? What's your Mom doing?" I asked.

Joanne blurted out, "I don't know, I'm not doing it, I'm not doing it, Mom, get him!"

"What are you seeing, Joanne?"

"Mom's carrying him away. I'm running after Mom and Michael. I'm shouting, 'What happened, Mama? What happened, Mama?' I'm not getting any answer at all, so I'm running after her."

"Okay, go into your Mom's emotions," I suggested.

"She's calm, she's happy, she has a smile on her face."

I said, "On the count of three, you'll know why he was under the water. One ... two ... three. Who was holding him under the water?"

Joanne said, sobbing, "It's my Mother! She held him under the water."

"Why did she do that, Joanne?"

"She felt it was the right thing to do. She felt he would die slowly and painfully of encephalitis and that she was doing him a favor."

Suddenly, Joanne's mood shifted into anger towards her mother. "How could she do this to me? This is outrageous. And I know there's no way I would dream up something bad about my mother."

I swiftly took Joanne to age four and had her go in on her emotions with her Dad and his feelings towards her. Her findings surprised her. "I looked at my Dad and there was this wall up. He was hovering in the background, looking at me, as if he didn't trust me because I knew something. What it was I don't know because obviously I'd blocked it out. I was in such trauma that I blocked it out completely. But, he didn't know that. He had no idea if I'd say something to someone else. I saw my Mom off to one side, really sad and depressed.

"When I was four, I went upstairs in our old house, and I saw my Dad holding my sister down. He was on top of her. My Mom calmly pulled me away. So my Mom knew that he was sexually abusing her little girl. What frame of mind could the poor woman have been in when she was holding my brother under water in the bathtub?

"When I was five, I saw the gun scene I drew in class. My Mom was pointing the gun at Dad and yelling, 'Get out of here!'

"I kind of knew that it had to do with him abusing my sister. Mom actually shot at my Dad but missed. I think he left the house for a maybe a week after this. I felt real good having him gone."

Later, Joanne told me, "Through the regression, I made the connection with my grandmother, and felt that she'd stepped in really strongly around that time. I don't know whether she knew what really happened with my brother and sister, but she knew something was wrong and took me in. I spent a lot of time with her around that time. That's probably why you said she was my spirit guide."

It's true. I relayed the message from her grandmother, "I've always been concerned about you and I vowed that I'd take care of you forever."

Joanne said, "I remember in your reading thinking, 'I don't have any feelings about my Grandma,' but I didn't remember those times with her until the regression. A lot of things came together through the reading and regression, even though at first, I had a hard time believing all this. But, my husband accepted it right away. Ever since he met me, he'd say things like, 'There's something about your eyes. You're the saddest person I've ever met.' So, when I told him of the regression, he said, 'There, I've always felt that there was some deep seated sadness in you.'

"I called my sister, Susan, who was four years older than me, the one who had been through the sexual abuse. She admitted to me that she had always had a funny feeling about Michael's death.

"When I called my sister, Eleanor, who is six years older than me, she believed it. She said that after Susan had mentioned she had been sexually abused, it brought to surface the fact that she had always had some strange feeling about sex and our Dad. She never pursued it but now that Susan had brought it out in the open, she thought that maybe he'd approached her at some point.

"Eleanor had been 11 years old when Michael died, and my questions started her thinking about it. What kind of way was that for our parents to handle our brother's death? All she could remember was we were not allowed to mourn. Nobody went to a funeral. It was like Michael was alive one day and dead the next. And our parents didn't ever want to hear another word about it from any of us.

"After all of this surfaced through my sessions, I kept asking, 'Why me?' All my life, I've felt that people walked all over me, that nobody treated me like a real person. I've always felt like a second-hand person. And through the regression I learned why. My parents cared so little for my feelings they felt free to kill my brother in front of me, to abuse my sister in front of me, and to have a gun fight in front of me.

"The regression answered the question I always had in my mind, 'What is it that makes me always feel that I let my sister down?' I had seen my father sexually abusing her and did nothing. No wonder I had such a deep-seated feeling of disappointing her!

"As the Chief of Police, my Dad was a very public figure, and I admired him for the way other people perceived him. But he led a dual life. His family life was rotten. He was never home. You could never approach him. He teased hurtfully. But, my whole childhood, I was so proud of him, I idolized him. I wanted to be like him because he was a public figure that everyone seemed to like. He was always on television and everybody in the neighborhood liked him. I probably repressed my hate and angry feelings for my father because I felt they were wrong feelings. How could I feel this way when everyone else respected him? The problem must be me."

Comments on Joanne

Joanne was one of the easiest subjects I've ever worked with, quickly going into an altered state of consciousness and going very deep.

She is a prime example of how a reading may lead to a regression—whether it be this life or a past life—which may lead to a clearing. They work together to help untangle the past! And until we untangle the past, it's almost impossible to move forward. In many ways, your past serves as an anchor until you release and let go of any negative memories of it.

Besides the obvious forgive-and-release process that Joanne needs to go through on a continuous basis, she needs to work on loving herself. When we love ourselves, people will perceive us differently. She feels on a cellular level that she's a "second-hand person." No wonder! She needs to take that childhood floppy disk out of her head and throw it away as if it were a Frisbee. Then put in a new floppy disk and program it with affirmations such as, "I am a lovable and loving being", and "I deserve loving relationships and I accept them now."

This is a case where mirror work (looking yourself in the eyes in the mirror and reciting affirmations on your self-worth) is essential. When looking into your own eyes in the mirror and saying these types of affirmations, you can heal years of others making you feel unworthy.

Acknowledge what is right with you every day and the good will grow.

Everything that happens is a lesson, and you either learn from it and grow, or become a victim of it. Joanne is growing!

Joanne also underwent a clearing in one of my monthly meditation groups. She later said, "I definitely had my dad in me. I've been hesitant about meeting up with him since I have a lot of negative feelings about him. As you were talking to his spirit, I felt overwhelming rage and anger. I definitely felt someone leaving me, although I had a couple of other spirits in me. I saw a baby leaving, and felt that I'd had my baby brother also in me."

"Yes," I replied, "I felt your brother was in you also. It makes sense since you were in the bathtub with him when he died. His spirit was frightened and jumped into you."

"I felt it was my brother that left, I felt my father stay."

"So did I."

Comments on Joanne's Clearing

This would have been better done one-on-one rather than in a group setting. Then, I would have persisted on getting her father to go on to the light. As it is, we'll do it in a private session.

It's sad to think how many years Joanne's baby brother has

been living through her instead of being on his own evolutionary path.

17. Mary Sue

Mary Sue had been coming to see me as part of uncovering her spirituality for almost a year before she had the most phenomenal experience. On July 1ˢᵗ, she called to make an appointment for a reading for Saturday, July 6th. On July 4th, she decided to write down her questions and remembered that an aunt had sent her some photos and family tree information about three months earlier. Here's what happened in her own words.

"I never knew my grandfather because he died four months after my mother was born, but I always had a feeling that he hadn't died as my grandmother had said. She'd always said he went into the hospital and died the next day.

"The package from my aunt contained photos of my grandfather, and I was shocked to see the striking resemblance between him and my ex-husband. The shape of the head, the smile, the eyes, and the hairstyle made them almost identical. Among the marriage and death certificates and photos was a picture of a woman who resembled me, and when I looked closely at the photo, I felt her soul. She was the mother of the grandfather who my ex-husband resembled. In the reading, I showed Marge the photo of the woman."

"Marge told that she saw that the woman died at age 34 of a self-induced abortion. The death certificate said this was in March, 1920. She was the mother of 11 children, Joseph was the oldest at 18 and Lena was the youngest, less than a year old when their mother died. She lived in New York and was married to a baker. Oddly, I went to culinary school in New York and have held positions as a pastry chef. I love to bake and she married a baker.

"I love my solitude and I have a fear of having children. She had 11 children and perhaps never had any solitude. I had an abortion when I was 20. She had an abortion in 1920. I get up every morning at 3:45 a.m. to go to work. She died at 3:45 a.m. I've always hated the month of March but was never sure why; she died in March. I was married and lived in Arizona; Lena, the youngest child, now lives in Arizona. I was married on September 22nd and Lena attended my wedding though I didn't even know who she was. My great-grandmother was also married on September 22nd.

When I saw the photo of her great-grandmother, I said, "You look just like her! You know that you're the same soul as your great-grandmother, don't you?"

Then I saw the photos of her grandfather and ex-husband, and immediately said, "They're one and the same soul. I also see your grandfather with a gun."

"That's intriguing. I've always felt that he was in the Mafia."

"It seems that he used it more to protect his family than for violence. Oh, that's interesting. Your ex-husband was your son in another past life. Is your ex-husband interested in guns? It seems to have carried over from the grandfather lifetime into this one."

"Just when I was getting ready to divorce him, he was getting more and more into guns."

"I see him becoming physically violent in this life because he has a lot of pent-up energy to release, most of which he brought from that past life."

Comments on Mary Sue

I have seen time and again how families come back together over and over again. In this case, Mary Sue was her own great-grandmother, and gave birth to the same spirit she married in a later lifetime. We come back often because of the strong love bonds we have together. But, also we come back to work off karma with each other that often spans multiple lives. This is why, if you don't get along with a family member or friend, you want to work diligently on forgiving and releasing them in this life. Otherwise the next time around this person may be your mother! If you hold angry and resentful feelings towards others and don't try to resolve them, then you'll need to come back in another lifetime with this person. Once is enough! Work it out through the forgive-and-release process.

Mary Sue and her great grandmother look almost identical, as do her grandfather and ex-husband, but it's not necessarily always so.

And finally, a numerologist would have a field day with the similarity in the numbers in this story. Numerology, like astrology, is a science. Again, there's no such thing as a coincidence.

18. Kristy

Kristy's father was diagnosed with cancer in May, 1991, and she came to me for a reading in March of 1992. Her father showed up immediately.

"Your Dad's Higher Self is here," I told her. "He's telling you that he is in a better space than you think. He sleeps a lot, and when he does, he's astral projecting over to the other side, preparing himself for the transition. He visits a lot with a brother he was real close to. In fact, the brother is on the other side, and is also here in the room with us.

"On the subconscious level, your Dad knows that when the time is right for him to cross over, his brother, Bill, is going to stand beside him and put his hand out. Then your father will simply step out of his body and Bill will welcome him to the other side.

"Your father feels no fear. He feels very secure. He wishes he felt this more on the conscious level so he could talk to the family about it. But it has not drifted down to his conscious mind.

"Your Uncle Bill is saying, 'Don't worry, Kristy, I'll show him the ropes. He has many highly evolved souls helping him to adjust.'

"I feel your Dad is going to have a peaceful, I want to say painless, death. When the time is right and the pain starts, Bill will come and say, 'Let's go!' I feel that it is going to happen when he is asleep.

"His Higher Self is saying, 'You're going to be extremely aware of him once he crosses over. Be open to receive and recognize his presence. Know that he is very content about the thought of crossing even though there is a sadness on the conscious level.'

"I'm hearing that he will only be bedridden for a week or two. Bill just added, 'There is a special place waiting for him.' "

Kristy later told me, "For the last ten days of Dad's life, he was bedridden and spent most of his time sleeping, as you predicted. He was on heavy painkillers at that time. On Sunday, June 21st, 1992, I was standing on one side of Dad's bed and my aunt Martha (uncle Bill's widow) was standing on the other side of his bed. We were talking quietly when Dad started getting very agitated and tried to get up. 'What do you want?' I asked him.

" 'Help me sit up so I can see Bill when he comes!' My aunt and I simply looked at each other, both of us knowing that the time was near and that he was waiting for his brother. I had told aunt Martha what you'd said in my reading about his brother Bill spending time with him. Dad slipped into a coma about ten in the morning on Tuesday, June 23rd, and crossed over three hours later. I know Uncle Bill was there to help him."

19. Donna

The first person who showed up for Donna's reading was a woman. "She's a thin, short lady with long, light brown, straight hair, and large, round, brown eyes. She looks to be around 27 years old. She's sitting in a rocking chair, holding a girl about 2-3 years old who has sandy to light brown hair. The lady is saying, 'I never left you.' "

At this, Donna started crying.

"What's the matter?" I asked.

"You just described my mother perfectly, She died of cancer

when I was 2 years old. I was really never very happy after that, being brought up by a cold, distant stepmother who I felt never loved me. I always wondered if my Mom was around me as I was growing up. Dad was always distant, too."

"There's a younger woman here, too. She hasn't crossed over yet."

When I described her, Donna said, "That's my daughter."

"Interesting," I said. "Did you know that she was your mother in a past life, and that she brought back her motherly tendencies towards you from that other lifetime?"

Donna burst out laughing. "She's always told me what to do and how I should do it, from the time she began talking. I'm going to give her one of your gift certificates for a telephone reading! You know, I'm over 50 and only wish I'd had this reading many years ago. You'll never know the joy and peace that my mother's message brings me."

Comments on Donna

How thrilling this must have been for Donna's mother to make this wonderful breakthrough after all these years. The veil between the two worlds is vanishing rapidly now, so this is a much easier process now than it was when Donna's mother crossed over. A lot of the earth's density and karma have been lifted in just the past three to four years, allowing more of the God light to penetrate onto our earth plane.

Today it's not unusual to hear people discussing their favorite psychic or reincarnation. But when I started over thirty years ago, if you talked about this, people thought your elevator didn't go all the way to the top floor. In fact, I called myself a "closet psychic." People knew me for years before realizing what I did.

As Donna lives in a different state, her reading was done over the telephone. For many years after starting my readings, I didn't realize I could do phone readings. But about twenty years ago, I first became aware of the spirit's sound over electrical wires. I realized that it was easy for them to communicate (at least their sound) using electricity. I have an intercom in my house that we never use. Often, if one of my guides or family members on the other side wants my attention, they use my intercom even though it isn't turned on.

Over electrical appliances, their sound comes through very loud. It's similar to the "popping" noises you here when you turn off your television and it's cooling down. I've heard that sound from my television when it hasn't been on for days. That's a spirit trying to communicate, trying desperately to get our attention.

Then, I found that when I'm on the phone with a client who says something that's not true, I literally hear another voice saying, "That's not true," or, I hear what the true story is rather than what the other person is saying. It can be distracting for me to talk on the phone because when you develop your sixth sense, you realize how many people lie.

Also, if someone on the phone is telling me about a problem they're having, I find myself spontaneously telling them how to deal with it. Of course, I'm getting information from their guardian angel, guide or higher self, via the electrical energies.

So, soon after I realized this, I started to do phone readings, and can see my client's deceased family and friends as easily over the telephone as I do when they are in the room with me.

Those on the other side will go to great lengths to get our attention. For example, when my Mom, sister and I used to meditate together, in the room with us, we'd have the guitar that used to belong to my brother Mick. He would often show up just to strum some chords for us.

20. Doug

Doug had come to me for a few readings because he was very unhappy and had searched for years for someone to help him to come out of the deep, depressive, fog-like state he'd suffered since he was 17 years old. He told me, "My parents had always attributed the dramatic change in my personality—from happy-go-lucky to withdrawn, depressed and moody—to the death of my dog who I'd had since my second birthday."

In the reading, I described the first spirit who showed up.

"That's my favorite aunt," Doug said.

"She's one of your spirit guides. She's telling me that you have several entities in you. One of these entities is causing all the negative happenings in your life."

That hit a nerve with Doug, who admitted, "After putting up with eight years of me being physically and mentally abusive to her, my wife just left me and took our two children. I physically abused them, too. She's in hiding from me because of my obsessive abuse."

"You know, Doug, we often pick up earthbound spirits at hospitals, cemeteries and mortuaries."

"That makes sense. We lived next door to a cemetery when I was seventeen. A few months after we moved in from out of state, my dog who was my best friend was struck by a car. He was killed instantly, right in front of me. I spent many hours by myself in the cemetery, just sitting there with my back against a tree, feeling very alone. It had been hard at seventeen to move away from all my friends and start all over. I felt peaceful at the cemetery. But, you're right. That was when all my problems started."

Doug continued, "It's about a three-and-a-half hour drive from my home to yours, and all the way here, I was hearing voices in my head calling you every filthy name I'd ever heard. Then, when that didn't work, they told me that I would die if I had this clearing. Looking back, I'm amazed that I kept driving to San Jose and didn't call to cancel our appointment.

During the clearing, I actually saw and felt two entities leave him immediately, but it took me a while to coax the third one to leave. It put up a lot of resistance, but finally it, too, left.

After the session, Doug did something strange. He jumped up and ran to my mirror. "What are you doing?" I asked, puzzled.

"It worked! It really worked!" he shouted excitedly.

"What do you mean?" I asked.

"For the first time in I don't know how many years, I can look at my face in a mirror. Until now, every time I've looked in a mirror, someone else was looking back at me through my eyes."

Comments on Doug

It's been a little over a year and a half since that clearing. Doug is now living with his girlfriend and her seven-year-old son. This is the first non-abusive relationship he's been in. In fact, he told me, "It's hard for me to imagine hurting anyone!"

21. Heather

Heather had been coming to me for readings off and on for about eight years. About 18 months ago, she started coming to my seminars and monthly meditation group. She had gone through a lot of loss in a short period of time. Her aunt, sister, mother, and mother-in-law had all died in the same year. A few months after that, her husband of 23 years left her for a woman the age of their daughters. It was a devastating time for her, financially, emotionally, and physically. Her husband left all his obligations behind, including his daughters and all the financial responsibilities.

Her friends told Heather that she needed counseling to get through, but she said stoically, "I'm just fine."

When she was a teenager, Heather had given up two daughters for adoption. After the divorce and a reading with me, she began to try to find them. Within a year, she found them both. While it had been a wonderful, happy experience, bringing up a past that had been hidden for so long was very emotional and stressful. Her immune system broke down and she contracted Epstein-Barr syndrome and became very ill.

In her search to be healed, she came back to me and decided to take my seminars to find some answers. This opened her up to the most healthy and spiritual time of her life.

Heather began our session with, "I'm here to ask you about my two daughters who I gave up for adoption. Up until now, I've never been able to talk about them, except to one close friend.

"When I was fifteen, I had my first daughter with Jeff, the man I ended up being married to for twenty three years. After we got married, I had two other children with him.

"I lived in a small town, and getting pregnant was very shameful. It was a very terrible thing to go through. I was in a home for unwed mothers, and he was in a home for troubled boys. So basically we broke up. He was ashamed of me and didn't want anything to do with me. When I had my daughter, Celise, I gave her up for adoption. It was terrible. I was heart-broken. Then I went back to school and became a student council officer. Getting active in the school was extremely good for me.

"Then I started to go with a boy who was a great guy. He was on the swim team, and I was student body treasurer. We were voted the cutest couple in school. I wouldn't do anything sexually with him until one night when we went to a party and I drank too much. We were together just one time and I got pregnant! So when I graduated from high school, I was student body vice-president and five months pregnant, which was also very shameful."

"I'm sure, especially in those times," I agreed. "Did your pregnancy show at the time of your graduation?"

"It was starting to, but I was able to hide it pretty well."

"Good."

"So I went to Monterey to have my baby—a girl, Carolyn. I almost didn't give her up. I basically had a nervous breakdown over that. That was really tough. I ended up coming back to Santa Maria, and the kids basically shooed me out of town."

"You mean your friends?"

"Yes, my 'supposed' friends. So I moved down to Los Angeles, and then Jeff, the father of my first daughter, came back into my life. We ended up getting married."

"How old were you then?" I asked.

"I was nineteen. A big part of the reason I married him was because he knew about my pregnancies. And besides, I felt I loved him. But he would never discuss my daughters, I couldn't tell anybody. So, all through the years, every time the girls' birthdays would come, I always had to stuff my feelings, and keep it all inside. Jeff would never let me talk about it with him."

"It's interesting that he wouldn't let you talk about it, being the father of one of them!"

"Oh no, as far as he was concerned, it never happened. Meanwhile, we had two daughters together while we were married. And then, after twenty three years of marriage, we ended up getting divorced."

"So why are you here today?"

"I came for a reading about the daughters I put up for adoption."

I was suddenly deluged with information. "Okay, one of them is in Los Angeles and the other's in Carmel. One daughter has just had a baby and she's often thought about looking for you. But now, that thought has kind of gone away."

Later, Heather told me, "After my divorce, I went to my twenty-five-year high school reunion by myself. It was my way of ending all this shame. I keep saying 'shame' because that's what I always felt. Going to this reunion was a giant step for me. On the way there, I turned around and came home a couple of times. But then I ended up going back and dealing with it. I went through a lot of pain for quite a while."

"Were your classmates still cruel to you?"

"No, they were fine, but it was opening up all the past. They were great. I don't even think they remembered. And yet I have vivid memories of every single thing that every one of them said to me or did to me. At the reunion, Glen, the father of my second daughter, sat me down and told me that all these years, he'd been thinking about our daughter and he wanted to find her. He asked if we could go about doing that. I agreed, of course. This started the ball rolling for me. I opened up the birth records on both girls."

"I thought that was hard to do."

"It is really hard to do. It was not easy. Actually the hardest part was that my first daughter, Celise, had already gone to get the records. They really gave her a hard time over getting my name. And then it turned out that the person she talked to ended up sending her everything, all the birth records, everything, then basically closed the file. This was after quite a long time of her trying to find out where I was."

"Was Celise the one I saw in southern California?"

"Yes, the first daughter. She had just had a little boy, he was three months old. She called me the day after Mother's Day. And, absolutely the moment we spoke, you could feel our bond right through the telephone wires. It was just very strong and still is very strong. Her and my two girls are very close to each other. If they were in a room together, you'd never know which two I raised and which one I didn't."

"Did she have a nice childhood?"

"It was okay. It wasn't great. She had a good father, but the relationship with her mother was strained. She and I have a very, very good relationship and I think we're going to get closer all the time. It makes it really nice. So that was in May of 1993.

"My youngest daughter, who I brought up, got married and Celise went to the wedding and my ex-husband never even said, 'Hello' to her or acknowledge her. But he knew who she was."

"Didn't she approach him?"

"She had called him on the phone and talked to him and he acted like, 'Yes, I can't wait to meet you.' But when she called him a couple of times after that, he wouldn't talk to her."

"How sad."

"But at the wedding, he also wouldn't speak to my twenty-four-year old daughter either—the one he raised. She, Celise, and my twenty-four-year-old are like best friends and sisters.

"Then, soon after, my second daughter, Carolyn, called me. Her adoptive mother had gone on the search for me. I'd met her parents as part of the adoption process, because I wasn't going to give her up unless I met them and saw the kind of people they were. Her adoptive mother remembered that I'd lived in Santa Maria, so she and her husband went there. They searched all the town records and asked questions all around town. Finally, they found someone who had been a good friend of my mother. That's how she found me."

"How nice of her parents to do this!"

"She's a wonderful, wonderful woman."

"Is this daughter, Carolyn, close to both of them?"

"Her father passed away when she was about ten. But she's very close to her mother."

"She must be very secure in herself to be able to look up the records for her adopted child."

"Yes, she told me that I'd given her the greatest gift she could have ever had, and how much she loved me. She's just that kind of a person. She told me that she could never have made it if it wasn't for Carolyn. It's just been incredible. I haven't yet developed a real relationship with her because I've been on this whirlwind. But I would like to because she's a great lady.

"Carolyn, too, is wonderful. She was raised in the Carmel area and then got married and moved to Utah. I have a granddaughter, Melissa, by her."

"Ah, yes. She's the one I saw psychically who wanted to find you when she had Melissa."

"Melissa's almost seven now. She's a real sweetheart. But I'll tell you, Marge, as wonderful as it is, it's been an emotional whirlwind to bring all this back up after all those years of not having talked about it. Then to have it all come at once was tough! It's hard for me to tell the story. I really still can't tell many people."

"A lot of that has to do with the era you were brought up in. The children today who have a child out of wedlock don't have to go through community shame as you did! Has Carolyn met Glen, her dad?"

"Yes, she has. The day after I found her, I called him. They have a great relationship. She talks to him a lot. She is very psychic. Both of them have a lot of my abilities. Since the day I found Carolyn, I've never spoken to her father again.

"My daughters that I brought up are doing great with all this news. They went around telling everyone because they were so excited. They were what got me to realize that it happened, and it's okay because I found my other two daughters.

"But it's largely due to you, Marge. It was knowing they were okay that made it all right for me to go ahead with the search. I had blocked a lot of it because I was afraid they weren't okay. Once I knew they were okay, it was like, 'Fine, now it can happen.' And it did!"

Comments on Heather

Everything happens for a reason. It was obviously time for Heather to move on from her marriage, find her first two children, and get onto her spiritual path. As often happens, ending the marriage and going through the pain that was involved spiraled her into going within and finding solace there.

When going through a situation like this, you need to affirm to yourself that there are no limits to the powers that you possess. Know that you are responsible for putting your own limits or blocks to your powers within. I've watched Heather blossom since her divorce. When you hold high thoughts about yourself and others, everything in your world blossoms. Low thoughts destroy. Your thoughts will lead you to being exactly the kind of person that you choose for yourself. Thought is the most powerful creative force in the universe. Know that your thinking shapes your lives. All that comes to you, good or bad, is caused by your thinking.

While going through the emotional pain right after the divorce, Heather found herself going from one illness to another. She found it almost impossible to lift her own spirits. If this happens to you, lift the vibrations in your home, and avoid being too serious. Loosen up and open up. Sometimes we can feel too responsible, too burdened down. Don't let your house become too heavy. Even if all adults live in your house, you need "kid stuff." You need to play. Lift the vibrations, get away from being too serious. I saw a plaque once that said, "Life is too important to be taken seriously."

Children are so happy, so uninhibited. We need to learn from them. They play and are so loving. We all need to lighten up. Don't lose your child within. We all need to play more.

Heather came back to deal with another issue in her life:

"The final issue I hadn't dealt with, (and didn't realize I needed to until recently at a reading with Marge) is that I was attracting men into my life who had either been very rich and had lost it all before I met them, or lost it all while I was with them. Was this me, I wondered, or just coincidence?

"In a reading, Marge saw that this was a past life problem that I'd carried over into this life. This led us to do a regression, and what really amazed me was that four days after the regression, I met a man who was completely different from the others. He is very 'healthy,' has a good sense of himself, and is very stable financially. We are very happy and have a wonderful time together. It's too early to tell if he's the person I'll marry, but the important thing is that I attracted someone completely the opposite of any other man I have brought into my life. I let go of the things that happened in my past lives and my present life and was able to move on."

Heather's Regression

After putting Heather in an altered state of consciousness, I took her back to a previous life. Following are some excerpts from her regression.

"You are ten years old. Where are you living?" I began.

"I'm living in a huge house."

"What does your dad do?"

"He's in some sort of banking and real estate. He seems to do all kinds of things."

"Look closely at your dad. Is he someone you know in this life?"

"Yes, he's my ex-husband."

"Are you close to your father?"

"No. I'm almost like a prize to him. He's very distant, very cold."

"Do you love your dad?"

"Yes."

"Look at your mom in that life. Is she someone you know in this life?"

"Yes, it's my aunt Michale."

"Are you close to your aunt?"

"Yes. She was a good mom. I know she loves me but she's kind of distant. I am really pretty."

"You're now age fifteen in that life. Have your subconscious mind and your higher self show you any significant events that have happened in the last five years."

"I'm happier at age fifteen than I was at ten."

"Let's go in on your relationship with your dad at age fifteen."

"I can't see him now."

"On the count of three, you'll now go back to the last day that dad was in your life. One ... two ... three."

"He left when I was thirteen years old." (Heather started to sob.)

"Let it come out, Heather. Don't try to stop your crying, that's very healing for you. Why did he leave?"

"He just walked out the door. He was very mad about something."

"Go in on the emotions of your mom at that time. What's happening with mom?"

"She's just sitting there with a smile on her face."

"Okay. Now we're going to go back to age fifteen. You'll see all the significant events that have happened since dad left."

"I'm actually happier now."

"Let's go in on the abundance issue. Did dad take all your abundance away when he left?"

"No. We had a lot of money but my life was like an empty shell.

We had everything we wanted materially but all the warmth was gone."

"I'm now going to take you through a 'forgive and release' process with your dad. See yourself as that thirteen-year-old, and visualize what your dad looked like the day he walked out that door. Now see a large balloon in the sky, make it any color you'd like. Put your dad in that balloon. See yourself as that thirteen-year-old. Go into that balloon.

"Now let's visualize a gold light around him so we don't hurt him (the color gold neutralizes negative thoughts). Tell him how hard, how awful it was for you after he left you, and how you felt like an empty shell. Tell him everything you felt. Hit him or kick him if you want. Whatever feels good. Bring up all those emotions you held inside in that life and brought over into this life. Let's get rid of that emotion of abandonment once and for all. (Because Heather sobbed earlier in this regression, it shows that she never dealt with the strong emotions of abandonment from that past life.)

"Now see yourself as that thirteen-year-old getting out of that balloon. But, before you do, look into your dad's eyes and say, 'I love you and I forgive you.' See yourself putting your arms around daddy and giving him a big hug. Mentally say, 'I forgive and release you with joy and ease and no struggle. Go on your way, dad, and be happy.'

"Now say to yourself, 'The past is over, I am free. The past has no power over me.'

"And now, while you're still in the balloon, see an umbilical cord from your heart to daddy's heart. Now see yourself cut this umbilical cord. Cut the cord! And now see yourself getting out of the balloon and standing on the earth. See your dad still up in that balloon. The balloon has a string attached to it and the other end of the string is attached to your heart, your thirteen-year-old heart. Once again, see the scissors cutting the string. Feel the release as your dad floats off into the universe, as you mentally say, 'I forgive you for walking away from me when I was only thirteen and making my life feel like an empty shell.'

"Now see yourself as that beautiful thirteen-year-old. See yourself facing yourself, Heather. Put your arms out to yourself and walk into your own arms. Feel your arms around yourself. Say to yourself, 'I am lovable. I am a loving child. It's not my fault that daddy walked out the door. It wasn't my fault. I forgive myself for wanting or needing that experience.' "

Heather did lots of crying while releasing her father from that past life. Crying is one of the most therapeutic things we can do for ourselves. It brings everything we've been holding inside all these years, all these lifetimes, up and out into the universe.

"Now see yourself in a tunnel, and you're now floating back into this life when you were married to that same man, to Jeff. At the count of three, you'll be back in this life. Number one: feeling yourself floating forward in time, forward, forward. Number two: you're coming forward in time, stretch, reach. Number three: you're back in this life. You're back in this life as that young girl when you met Jeff again.

"This same person came into your life, this time as your ex-husband, and he was making big money, and then he left you. You are immediately attracted to him, and your subconscious mind remembers that he was your daddy before, and you loved him so much. You want another chance to get him to love you this time. You're going to give him another chance this time to have money with you but not walk away and leave you as an empty shell. You are giving him another chance to work off this karma with you.

"Unfortunately for Jeff, it didn't quite work out that way. So, we are going to come forward in time. Forward in time to the day that Jeff walked out your door in this life, when once again, you had great abundance. And again in this life, you felt that you couldn't be happy after he left you. Let it out, Heather, once and for all. Put him in a balloon and tell him how you feel. Take your time. He did the same thing to you in this life!"

I then led Heather in a forgive-and-release process with her husband in this life, Jeff. It had been a repeat performance with Jeff. He had money again in this life and walked out on Heather, again leaving her an empty shell. One more time, he "did it to her." I helped her to release Jeff so that she would have no more fears of bringing wealthy men into her life.

Heather learned that the only reason this happened a second time in her life was because her father/husband wasn't strong enough to overcome his karma from a past life. This is not Heather's karma; it's Jeff's karma. I had her tell this to Jeff while she was in a balloon with him.

Once Heather knew this was carried over from the past, had nothing to do with her, and was a second chance for him, she was able to completely put it out of her mind (conscious and subconscious) and release it.

It took her two lifetimes, but she is finally free of Jeff, finally free from being made to feel "an empty shell." Both her father and Jeff gave her money but in neither lifetime gave her what she needed most of all—love and support. She never received unconditional love from them. In both lifetimes, she was a "prize," a "trophy." The karmic ties are gone because of this process; they will never have to come back together.

After Heather forgave herself one more time, I saw her standing in a meadow, much thinner than she was, and saw that her weight was going to just fall off her now that she finally had gotten to the source, to the core of why she put weight on—to protect herself. In the next three months, Heather lost 35 pounds without dieting.

The subconscious mind works in mysterious ways. Money in both of these lives did nothing but make her feel like an empty shell in the end. So even though on the conscious level, Heather would like to have money, her subconscious mind kept reminding her that twice now, she's been unhappy after having money. So, she has been magnetizing men into her life who have tremendous abundance problems.

While Heather was still in her altered state of consciousness, I had her repeat the following affirmations: *From this day forward, my weight will start to fall off of me...I do deserve abundance... I am loving and lovable... I deserve a loving, kind, fun relationship and I accept it now... I'm now magnetizing a man into my life who is very secure with himself... I am now magnetizing a man into my life who has abundance to share with me.*

I had her visualize the word FEAR in great big print and put the word in a balloon high in the sky. Once more that balloon had a string attached to it, and the other end of the string attached to her heart. I had her visualize herself with a pair of scissors and cut the string and watch the balloon with her fears in it drift off into the universe.

The key to becoming emotionally healthy is to release the past.

22. Lorraine

When Lorraine came to me for a reading, I described for her the first visitor.

"That's my ex-husband," she protested. "What is he doing here? I've been divorced from him for thirteen years and he's still terrorizing me!"

I smiled and said, "It would be interesting sometime to see your past life connection with him." I then continued on with the reading.

My remark haunted Lorraine because about two weeks later, she made an appointment for a regression. Here's what happened:

"I see myself born to my same mother in this life, but my father in this other life is someone I met at work this time around, someone I don't like that much. I seem to have a happy enough childhood.

"Now I'm five years old and my parents have just had a little boy. Guess who he is. Yes, he's my ex-husband in this life. For whatever reason, my parents are almost sadistic with him. They beat him frequently. Unfortunately, rather than feel sorry for him, I get caught up in their negative energies. I start telling my parents lies about him for the sheer joy of seeing him punished. They often draw his blood with these beatings.

"It's a hot day and we're both out swimming in a swimming hole. We're both excellent swimmers. He's quite close to shore when he has a tremendous cramp. I'm the only one in earshot, and he's yelling to me for help. I just stand on the shore and let him drown. No wonder he's terrorizing me in this life."

Comments on Lorraine

Once again, the puzzle pieces fit together. Lorraine was among one of the first people I ever regressed. About an hour after she got home, she phoned me and said, "I can finally get on with my life."

I said to my husband, "If I never do another regression, this is the most rewarding thing I've ever done." I've now done countless regressions and 99 percent of the time, they're this rewarding and revealing.

Lorraine's parents' attitude towards their son was obviously a past life connection with the three of them. I saw definite karmic ties there. We didn't pursue that, as it wasn't pertinent to Lorraine's connection to her brother or ex-husband in this life.

I helped her with forgiving herself while she was still in the energy of that past life. It's no wonder her brother brought into this life a lot of anger and resentment towards her. She needs to keep forgiving herself and sending him (her ex-husband) the God light. The God light dissipates all hatred, resentment and anger. She needs to charge herself with the God Light and then pulsate her God light out of her heart and see it entering his heart and filling his body.

This case is a perfect example of what karma is all about. She needed to be with him again in this lifetime to make up for her past-life mistakes. "What comes around, goes around," or "As you sow, so shall you reap." Once we see the bigger picture, everything makes sense.

If she would have just kept responding to her husband "terrorizing" her, she would have stayed stuck in her own story. If you respond to the garbage going on around you, you keep it there.

Often when you have a negative relationship, that person's in your life to tell you that you need to expand. Don't give a lot of power to them.

If their awareness is very limited, you may have drawn him or her to you to tell you that you need to increase your own awareness. As soon as you work on your own awareness, the agreement will have been kept, and he or she will go away.

23. Tamiko

Tamiko attended one of my public sessions, and when she heard me describe my work and how we can contact people who had passed over, she knew it was important for her to have a reading. Her father had died in the spring of 1987, and she'd suspected that they'd communicated briefly but then told herself, "Oh, that's just my imagination!"

Tamiko told me, "Before he died, I felt incomplete in our relationship. I really loved my father all my life. Yet especially when he was older, I felt he didn't understand me. He seemed to be trying to get me to be 'saved' the way he thought I should be. I just felt he couldn't or didn't want to understand my spiritual path.

"About two weeks after he died, I was driving to work and found myself mentally talking with him, asking his forgiveness for my not being able to speak with him more clearly about his physical condition before he died even though I'm a medical doctor. And I had the sense that, of course, he understood now and that he really loved me. But, I told myself, "Oh that's just my wishful thinking."

In her reading, the first spirit who came was, of course, her father. When I described him, she said, "Yes, that's a perfect match."

"He's telling me to tell you, 'I *do* understand your spiritual path now, and furthermore, I want to help you in your personal life because by helping you, it will help me to grow, too. But, you have to *ask* for my help. It is very important for you to learn to ask for help.' "

Another spirit came through whom I described. "She's my favorite aunt, she's still living on this side." (Tamiko was surprised that the living could also come through.)

"She wants to tell you that she's ill, and that she's not sure at this time whether she wants to pass over or not. Her higher self is asking you to contact her."

Tamiko was really surprised by this because she had no idea her aunt was sick, but within two weeks, Tamiko's mother told her that her aunt was deeply depressed and was being put on medication.

Comments on Tamiko

Tamiko's reading involved her father, from the other side of the veil, telling her that she needs to ask for his help.

If you believe in reincarnation, you then know that we grow through our "lessons" here on earth, we grow most through our relationships. We magnetize certain people to us so we can learn and grow from their interaction with us. Because we literally draw these people to us, our guides are not allowed to "interfere" and counsel us unless we ask for their guidance. We draw people to us for whatever lessons they have to teach us as stepping-stones. Unfortunately, these lessons often become stumbling blocks instead of the stepping stones that we had intended. So, when we're in trouble of any kind, we need to ask for help.

Personally, I call for help on a daily basis. I even ask for guidance before I get out of bed in the morning! I ask for strenth, protection and guidance.

Finally, remember, dying doesn't make someone smarter. In meditation, visit with your loved ones on the other side, but for guidance, go right to the top. Ask God, your higher self, your guardian angel or your guides.

24. Amber

"On June 18, 1988, my daughter Jeanette, age 25, was murdered, and her body was dumped in Skaggs Island Waterway, about 10 miles

west of Vallejo, California. The last day I saw my Jeanetty alive was the previous evening and just three days after she gave birth to a baby girl. The pain I felt is indescribable. The pain has stayed with me because I'll never see her, hold her, or hear her voice again. So I thought!

"A friend told me about you, and said that the things you said struck him as being incredibly on target. He told me that you actually give readings over the phone and gave me your number so that I could call for a reading. Little did I know what I was going to hear and learn."

"You can ask any questions you want to, about anyone on this side or the other side, or I can just tell you who comes to speak to you."

"Why don't you tell me if anyone's here," Amber said tentatively.

"Well, there's an older lady," I said and described her. "And she's giving me her first initial, it's the letter 'L' "

"That's my grandmother, Lillian."

"There's someone else."

"He's my stepfather, Papa."

After a few family pleasantries, the accuracy of which blew Amber away, her murdered daughter showed up.

"I'm seeing a young girl, about average height, small frame, long brown hair, blue eyes. She's on the other side."

At that point, I had a hard time breathing, like I was choking. "Jeanette was strangled or suffocated, wasn't she?" I asked.

"Yes," Amber said faintly, and began to cry over the phone. Then she asked, "Will you tell Jeanette how much I miss her, how much I love her."

The phone suddenly had all kinds of static, and I asked Amber, "Are you on a portable phone?"

"No," she replied.

"That's weird. My phone never makes that sound. Maybe you'd better hang up and call me back. I hope we'll get a clearer line."

That's when I heard it, and so did Amber. As clear as could be, we heard Jeanette whisper, "I LOVE YOU"! Amber heard it two more times, but I only heard the static. The only time during our hour-long reading that we heard static was when Jeanette whispered to her mother.

"I'm also seeing that Jeanette is around her children all the time, and that after Jeanette has gained some strength on the other side, at least one of her children will become aware of her presence."

Amber later told me that this did happen. "My husband and I adopted two of Jeanette's children, Kevin, aged 9, and Mandy, aged 3. One Saturday morning, Kevin was playing soccer with his school team against another school. Kevin's team wasn't doing too well, so I looked up a little and said, 'Come on, Jeanette, that's your son out there and he needs help. How about getting out there and guiding him?"

"Just then, Kevin worked the ball all the way down the field and scored a goal. After the game, Kevin whispered to me (he calls me Mom), 'Mom, I heard mommy talking to me out there! I really did hear her!' And she heard me, just as you had predicted."

Halfway through another reading about four or five months later, I told Amber, "Close your eyes and relax. Jeanette's going to give you a big hug."

She said, "I can actually feel the pressure of someone giving me a big hug. I know it's Jeanette." She started crying and said, "I can feel it, it's her, Jeanette, giving me a big hug. Thank you, Marge, for bringing my little girl to me, even if it was brief, it was GREAT!"

25. Michelle

Michelle's grandmother had been to me for a regression and then a reading. At the reading, I described her granddaughter who, I saw, had a young female spirit attached. They were at the scene of an accident where a girl on a bike had been struck by a car and killed.

I saw that Michelle had been close behind on her bike, and that in the fright, panic and commotion surrounding her accident, the dead girl's spirit simply stepped into Michelle's body. I could see clearly that this spirit had been adversely affecting Michelle ever since.

The grandmother told me that her college graduation present to Michelle was a cycling trip through Europe. Just outside Paris, two girls on bikes about twenty feet in front of Michelle were hit by a car. One died instantly; the other was seriously injured.

After that incident, Michelle's personality changed completely. Her occasional use of alcohol escalated rapidly and she was diagnosed as a schizophrenic. She often heard voices in her head, many times arguing with her. She would often feel her mouth moving, as if someone was trying to talk through her. She couldn't hold down a job, mainly because of a very short attention span.

In the session, I told Michelle, "This sounds like a classic case of possession."

"What's that? You mean like in the movie *The Exorcist*?"

"Not usually that dramatic," I said, smiling.

"Well, I'm here at my grandmother's insistence. I guess I've nothing to lose."

After the preliminaries, I addressed the spirit in Michelle, and called to her friends and relatives on the other side to help lead her to the light.

Afterwards, Michelle said, "I felt all kinds of physical sensations, like energy running up and down my spine. I think I briefly 'saw' the spirit, but it's hard for me to say what I felt when she left me. I guess the best way I can describe it is that I felt as if a light breeze went through my body, and I felt 'lighter' somehow."

Michelle told me recently, "It's been two and a half years since that day in your office. I stopped drinking any form of alcohol soon after. I just lost my taste for it from that day forward. I don't hear any voices in my head. It's great not to feel like I'm arguing with myself, and my mouth only moves when I want it to. And I've been in one job since. Now that's a record for me."

Comments on Michelle

I firmly believe that many people have been locked up in mental institutions, when all they needed was a clearing, which takes me only about half an hour to do!

26. Pat

Following is an account of one of my many experiences with spirits on the other side. The last member of my own family who crossed over was my only sister, Pat. It's still devastating to lose anyone, but when you develop your sixth sense—and believe me, we all have it—and become aware of their presence, or better yet, contact them, it helps tremendously to transcend the grief.

It was Saturday morning, February 9th, 1991, and I was up in the Napa Valley wine country giving my "Beginning Your Intuitive Search" weekend seminar. The class was interrupted by the message that I had an emergency phone call from my daughter, Barbara. She told me that I needed to get home if I wanted to see my sister alive.

In hindsight, I realize that I went into shock, but feeling obligated to my clients (one of them had driven all the way down from Oregon), I continued with the seminar, promising to check back with my daughter during the lunch break.

I threw myself into the seminar and didn't allow myself time to dwell on my phone call. After all, Pat hadn't even been sick. Just the week before, she had danced almost every dance at her son's wedding.

After class, on the two-and-a-half-hour drive to the hospital around seven that evening, I felt Pat's presence in the car with me. I asked her to hold on until I got to the hospital. When I arrived, she was purple, in a coma, and extremely bloated. I saw her floating near the ceiling, feeling very confused.

"If it's your spirit's will, go to the light," I told her.

Vanishing Veil

The previous afternoon, she'd gone shopping with one of her daughters. When she came home, she went to bed saying she didn't feel well. When her husband arrived home from work, he checked on her, but she was sleeping. The next morning, he woke up at five and she was out of bed, so he went to check on her. She was sitting in her favorite chair in the family room. She said, "When the clinic opens at eight, I think I should go in and be checked.

Her husband said, "No, we're not going to wait for the clinic to open, I'm taking you to the hospital emergency room."

He wheeled her into the emergency room in a wheel chair and she immediately went into a coma from which she never came out.

Very early Sunday morning, I left the hospital and drove back to finish my seminar. At five in the morning, I received a call from my husband saying that Pat had crossed over. As difficult as it was, I finished giving my seminar, did a few readings, and went home. Once back, I tried automatic handwriting. I put Pat's name at the top of a piece of paper and asked her, "What do I most need to know at this time?"

Pat wrote (through my hand) "Just keep on your path, don't look back."

Ten days after she crossed over, I received the following message from her through automatic writing, "Hi, Marge, I want to thank you for my funeral dinner. It's hard to imagine I'm here. You're right, how you think of life over here. Dad and Jerry (my first husband) are with me. Stephen (my second child) will come to Laura (my oldest daughter). Write your book—lots of case histories. I didn't suffer, I'm okay. It's hard to leave a family. I guess it would be hard at any time. I'm pure energy now! Thanks for telling me to go to the light. I was confused."

For the first two to three months after her passing, I felt her presence a lot. I also saw her many times and had numerous telepathic conversations with her.

One of her daughters came for a reading within the first year of Pat's crossing. Throughout her reading, we heard loud 'clicking' noises that were so loud that I almost doubted it was Pat, and thought my new tape recorder was acting up. She definitely wanted her daughter to know it was her. (My tape recorder has never made that noise before or after that reading.) Also, Pat's energy jumped into me and cried through me. She was so emotional, but happy, at making such a strong contact with her daughter.

My Mom came over for a day to help me bake some Christmas cookies. Right before dinner, we both went into the living room to relax. It was dark and the Christmas tree lights were on. Suddenly, I felt Pat's energy enter me. She cried uncontrollably through me. This was her first Christmas on the other side, and I shared her overwhelming sadness.

After dinner, my husband, Rob, went to watch television in the game room downstairs. Mom and I lingered over our dinner plates. Suddenly, Mom started choking and turning blue. A piece of food had lodged in her throat and she couldn't breathe. My first thought was to call Rob, but I knew he wouldn't make it upstairs in time. I mentally called to Pat since she'd taught nursing while on the earth plane. I saw her go up behind Mom and put her arms around her and squeezed in the right spot. A piece of food shot out of Mom's mouth! Immediately, she started breathing normally. They truly can help us even though they're on the other side of the veil.

On the first anniversary of Pat's death, I meditated immediately upon waking, as Pat was very much on my mind. I saw her with one of my Grandmas (also on the other side). Grandma (who Pat was very close to while on the earth plane) told me, "Don't worry, Pat's fine. I am making sure of that."

In March 1992, at my monthly meditation group, I was discussing how spirits can become one with us, live through us, and enjoy life through us. I was relating how, at a wedding shower for my niece at my house, I was talking to Pat's husband when I suddenly realized that Pat was talking to him through me. As I was discussing this with the group, we all heard the loudest 'click' ever.

I felt Pat's presence so strongly that tears came into my eyes. The 'click' was her way of affirming what I was saying.

When Pat's daughter called me to say she had been accepted at the college of her choice, I saw Pat standing in front of me, wearing the dress she bought for her son's wedding. She looked proud enough to burst and was absolutely beaming.

27. Trisha

Trisha had been coming to me on and off for readings to contact friends and relatives who had passed over. The readings were always touching and personal, until one day, she appeared for a reading distraught. She told me that a close friend had just died and that she was really upset. Unknown to both of us, that reading was about to change Trisha's life.

A young man showed up immediately and I described him to her.

"That's Mike," she confirmed, in between sobs.

Without more ado, Mike started explaining to Trisha. "I've always had gay tendencies but fought them all my life. I didn't tell you because I didn't want it to be real."

I had no idea what Mike was talking about, but it seemed meaningful to Trisha because she replied, "You died of AIDS three weeks after the wedding. What's it like to have AIDS?"

Mike explained, "It's the most horrible thing I've experienced. It was like I was dying piece by piece. Other friends I know who'd already died of AIDS helped me leave my body behind. They put their hands out to me and pulled me over to the other side. I didn't mind leaving my stiff, hard and tired body there."

"How do you feel now?" Trisha asked.

"I'm still really confused and really tired."

I could feel his tiredness. Mike talked very slowly and I could feel him forming the words, as though he was exhausted.

"I'm going to try and figure out what I'm going to do. There's a lot of work to do over here, and I'll probably help other AIDS patients cross over to this side. I've had a lot of time to think about it, but I still need to get more rest before I can do that. It's really special to me that I can talk to you like this, and I want you to know that I love you. You must trust that you're really hearing me, and you will become even more aware of me in the future."

Trisha then told me, "The day after I heard Mike had crossed over, I was in the kitchen, bent over on the kitchen counter crying. Suddenly I felt a very strong energy come up through my spine into me, and the thought that crossed my mind was that it was Mike, but I'd never heard of that happening. I've had that same feeling several times since then and have known it was him."

"Yes, that was me in the kitchen," Mike told me.

After a pause, Mike continued the message for Trisha, "We never ever were separated, and we have always been together. At night, we used to fly astrally together and be with each other although you may not remember it. When my higher self was deciding whether to cross over early, our higher selves met together and we discussed it. We agreed that if I did cross over earlier than I had originally intended, it would put you on your path sooner. We talked about how I would be able to help you and therefore grow more spiritually on the other side because I wasn't satisfied with my spiritual growth this time around. We knew that my death would catapult you on your path, that it would shake you up so much that there'd be no turning back."

"And, it did," Trisha agreed. "It was an extreme shock to me, to my system."

"I can't tell you how pleased I am to come through like this. You can't imagine how thrilling it is, especially after having just crossed over. It's so frustrating to want to talk to everyone you left behind and most of them don't hear a thing. You will grow spiritually because of my crossing. You will be amazed at how aware you'll become, how you'll trust your intuition because of me over here. If you have any problems, just ask me for help. I can help, but you must ask because we are not allowed to interfere unless you ask us."

Mike's energy was fading, so we ended the reading. I asked Trisha, "What was that all about?"

"I guess I need to explain who Mike was. I knew him in high school. His best friend was my cousin and the three of us did everything together. I often felt that Mike didn't like, that he even hated me. I often felt that I challenged him, but over the years we developed a special relationship. We shared what we read, what we wrote and what we thought. We both had difficult childhood and teenage years. We both felt very estranged from our families and he supported me in what I went through with my parents. My dad was emotionally abusive and he and Mike did not hit it off. Mike used to stand up to my dad and tell him he was looking at life all wrong, and my dad didn't care for that very much. So they were always at odds with each other.

"I was crazy about Mike but nobody knew it because I kept all my feelings inside. I was a very withdrawn person, very much to myself and had suppressed the memories of abuse early in my childhood.

"I was very unhappy and didn't feel alive, and Mike made me feel alive. He was fun-loving and everything he did made me laugh. I admired him because he was very, very smart. He could write better than I could, and I thought he would be a great writer. He was an okay student in the first two years of high school but then he did a turnaround and started getting straight A's. He would set an impossible goal for himself and meet it. We kind of had a brother-sister relationship where we would bicker. He would get mad at me for something and would leave me alone, only to suddenly show up in my life again.

"He was a year older than I was, and should have gone off to college but instead he decided to stay behind a year and get a job. He went to work for my dad, which seemed really unlikely. We went out together, never thinking of it as dating. We were really close but it wasn't until we were freshman in college that we actually had a romantic relationship. It only lasted three or four months but I felt like the happiest person in the world, and that we were really happy.

"Over time, however, he became distant from me and I blamed myself. When I confronted him, we had a very ugly scene, and we didn't see each other after that. At the time, it felt really final to me and I just wanted to die.

"Several months later, a friend of his told me that everyone was surprised we'd gotten together because Mike was gay. I was devastated, and it didn't make sense. It was all so confusing.

"About a year later, I met Herb and a year and a half later, we got married. I always thought Mike would come back to me but he never did. I saw him again years later at my cousin's wedding. We talked through the whole reception but there were so many things I didn't get to ask him, so many unresolved things for me that I've tortured myself for years after. Three weeks after the wedding, Mike died of AIDS.

"All the years that I was married to Herb, when Mike and I had lost contact, I remember periodically waking up startled and feeling Mike standing there smiling. Every time this happened, I always felt that he would just show up on my doorstep like the old days, and I would get ecstatic, like a little child.

"As time went by, Herb couldn't understand what I was going through and was actually jealous of Mike. I felt a tug of war going on at all times, and I was very confused."

A few months later, Trisha came back for a regression. Mike appeared once more and explained to her, "There was a lifetime where Herb and I were best friends and we were both in love with you. You chose me and Herb became very withdrawn, and angry and bitter. He died a very bitter old man."

In the past-life regression, Trisha saw this relationship. In her own words:

"Mike and I got married and what surprised me was that I died very young. When I was thirty-two, I died of pneumonia. We had been very happy and when I saw myself on my deathbed, I became extremely emotional because I saw Mike standing there at my bed and all I could think of was that it was too soon to go, that I wasn't ready yet to cross over. I saw that after I died, I watched over him and our kids because he was very upset and he had a very hard time with my crossing. A friend of mine in that life came to help him and they got married. I saw how I helped make this happen from the other side.

"In another lifetime, I saw that Mike and I were brother and sister, and our dad was the same one I have in this life. Our dad was very abusive to me both physically, mentally, and sexually, as he was in this life also. Mike was very protective of me just like he was in this life, always trying to shield me from my dad.

"Mike and I had a very deep love for each other and it didn't seem wrong to be together sexually, but when I got pregnant with Mike's baby, our dad made him go away into the military. I only saw Mike once after that. My dad made me marry an older man who I didn't care for but I had no choice. I really just wanted to die. The interesting thing is that the man dad married me off to was Herb in this life. He was very good to me and cared about me. The child Mike fathered is my cousin in this life, and was Mike's friend.

"My second child in that life was the daughter I have now, but I favored the little boy since he came from the man I loved. I rejected my husband in that life and didn't want his child, my daughter. I didn't want anything to do with him. I became the bitter, angry, unforgiving one in that life and he tried hard to keep it all together. This has a definite bearing in my present life because it is the reversed situation. Even though I feel Herb's caring, he holds back from me and is very bitter.

After the regression, Trisha told me, "After Mike's death, I left Herb. I just couldn't be with him anymore, he couldn't understand my feelings. He became even more angry, bitter and withdrawn, much like in his past life. I prayed for him not to go down that lonely path, not to become that lonely and bitter old man I saw in the regression. It's like we are reliving that life all over again when Mike and I were together, as if we're trying to replay it again."

In a later reading, I saw Mike merge with Trisha. He walked towards her and into her and I could actually see them both together, both of their faces, all of their features there at the same time. It was really beautiful for Trisha to know they were as one. She could feel this as I described it. She later told me that on the night after that reading, she'd gone to bed and asked about her other guides.

"Even though I felt myself laying in bed, I also felt myself leave and go somewhere that was higher and darker, with no walls. I saw a big ring of spirits, people I've known in this life who have died. There must have been two dozen of them, their faces aglow in white light. They looked so peaceful and so wonderful, not a worry in their faces. I saw my grandmother and we cried together. Some other friends told me, 'We tried to help you when you were younger but we didn't feel like we could intervene. But we want to help you now. All you have to do is ask.' I felt very close to all of them, it was wonderful."

Trisha continued, "I am currently in therapy for sexual abuse by my father and in two past lives, he also sexually abused me. Mike is very protective of me and tried to keep us apart. Once I started therapy, I began to see pictures in my head of myself being molested by my father when I was three or four. I thought I was making it up, so I came to see you, and when you regressed me back into early childhood in this life, I saw that it was true. It explained a lot of things, like I remember looking at pornographic material as a child and could never figure out where it came from. I believe now that my dad was showing it to me."

In Trisha's readings, Mike confirmed that her father had abused her and that her mother knew. Her dad hasn't overcome his problem yet and has spent time at a mental institute for recovery. However, he said he thought it was just a waste of time. This was a golden opportunity to clear out some old karma but he didn't take advantage of it.

Trisha has also taken classes with me that have helped her tremendously, especially the visualization techniques and how to send telepathic messages. They came in handy when she left her husband. In her own words:

"I got a job but told them that I would need a raise after three months. During the third month, I kept projecting into my boss' head, 'Trisha is worth more money.' At the end of the month, he offered me more than I'd asked for, and told me I'd have another raise at the end of the year!"

Comments on Trisha

Mike told Trisha how frustrating it was to try to communicate with family and friends still on the earth plane because they don't hear. That is one of many reasons for learning to meditate. As I stated earlier, Edgar Casey once said, "Praying is talking to God; meditating is listening to Him."

You can get so much guidance through meditation and also visit with loved ones who have crossed over, while in the meditative state (or altered state of consciousness).

With her relationships with Mike and her husband, Herb, it was important for Trisha to follow up the readings with the regressions into past lives to fully comprehend their relationships in this life. Mike's death propelled Trisha to go within for her answers, and she progressed rapidly on her spiritual path after his crossing, just as Mike had predicted.

Notice how we keep coming back with the same people? We come back with some because of our deep-seated love for them, but with many (as with Trisha's father), we keep coming back until we get it right or until the other person gets it right. The only way to stop this continuing nightmare for Trisha is for her to forgive and release her Dad completely and totally this time around.

Forgiving and releasing others is one of the most important things we can do for our spiritual progression. Even if a person is behaving despicably, we need to forgive and release them. We're not condoning their behavior and might never need to see them again, but we do need to forgive and release their higher self, their

God within. That we can all do.

Until Trisha fully forgives and releases her dad, she'll attract men into her life that have some of her father's characteristics, or men that won't stay in her life because her conscious mind and her subconscious mind will be fighting. Her conscious mind may think she wants a man in her life, but her subconscious mind will be saying, "No you don't. Look what one did to you when you were little!" This is the universe's way of telling her to deal with the source of her problems—her dad.

Times of turbulence, in which things are changing, offer much opportunity for growth. Many of us begin more actively seeking our spiritual growth during times of crises and change, as Trisha did. The energies hitting the earth right now will energize and activate whatever you are focusing on. For those of you who are sensitive and already focusing on your spiritual path, these new energies will make things work out better than ever before. Doors will open. You'll find yourself looking inward, finding the answers you've been searching for.

As you grow spiritually, you'll find it is time for your normal reality to be updated. You may need to change the job or relationship you have, as Trisha did. And there may be personal issues that you need to act upon and resolve. However, by making the changes you need to make in the real world, you will ultimately strengthen your spiritual growth.

Getting in touch with your own guides points you in the direction of your aliveness and growth, pinpointing such things as jobs you've wanted to leave or relationships that no longer nurture you. As you let go of the old and receive the new, you may go through some temporarily difficult times, but once you let it go, your life will dramatically improve. You'll have more abundance, love and success. Appreciate your lessons now as they come and know that they are preparing you to handle a higher vibration.

So many of us hang onto the worn-out shells of relationships, long after the life energy has left the connection. If you hang onto relationships after they're of use to you, you'll find yourself living in a heavier, harder energy, one of more struggle. If you're filling your time with an unsatisfying relationship, then there is no room in your life for a fulfilling one. And if a relationship dissolves, it simply means that it's time to move on. If it's time for one partner to move on, it's also time for the other one, too, even though he or she may not yet know it on a conscious level.

I was brought up believing, "Until death do us part." Now I say to my clients, "To the death of what? If it's the death of the marriage, it's time to move on." We didn't come to earth to be victims, to be abused sexually, mentally, verbally or physically. Neither did we come to be betrayed by our partner—trust and love go hand-in-hand. If you find yourself in this sort of situation, go into an altered state of consciousness and ask your angels and/or guides to show you the bigger picture. See what it is that you are to learn from this relationship. Learn it, forgive and release it and move on. Don't let yourself get caught up in a victim role.

Act upon your guides' whispers before they become shouts. Make the changes that your inner self, your God within, suggests to you.

28. Sam

Sam's cousin came to me for a reading, and I described a man who showed up even though he was still on this side of the veil.

"That's my cousin, Sam," he exclaimed.

"I don't know why he's here," I said, "but he's recently divorced from a women who is a very heavy drinker. He has two children, and his daughter is taking the breakup of her family extremely hard. I'm picking up very unhappy, almost negative, vibrations from her. And I see him remarrying."

Because of the accuracy of my descriptions, Sam decided to have a phone reading with me even though he was still very skeptical.

In Sam's reading, I answered his questions about his children and work, and then I saw an attractive lady coming into his life.

When I'd finished describing her, Sam asked, "Do you mind if I put the phone down and do cartwheels around the room?" Then I saw Sam's best friend and described him. "You just described my best friend to a tee."

"I see the two of you out to dinner at a nice restaurant with a small dance floor. You're asking this attractive lady to dance. You'll know it's her because she'll have an eight-year-old daughter."

I went on to describe the restaurant, its floor plan, and where they would be sitting. "Oh, and I see you rushing to the phone to call me and tell me about meeting her."

A couple of months later, Sam called me in a very excited state, and said, "My friend and I decided to treat ourselves to a night out on the town. After a delicious dinner, the music was so great that we decided to stay and dance. I asked this attractive gal to dance and halfway through our second dance, I realized that she looked exactly like the woman you described me meeting. So I'm sure you know what I did next! Of course, I asked her, 'Do you have any children?'

"She said, 'No, but I have an eight-year-old cat who I call Daughter!' Oh, and by the way, the restaurant had the exact floor plan that you'd seen!"

29. Celeste

Celeste came to see me because she was upset that the man she was dating, Jerry, kept leaving her. This brings up the abandonment issue that so many people have to deal with on one level or another.

In the reading, I immediately saw that Celeste had abandonment issues from past lives and early childhood. "Unless you deal with these issues, you'll keep attracting men into your life who won't stay. I suggest we do a few regressions and release the past."

I asked Celeste's higher self to take us to a past life that had a bearing on this issue. Here's what Celeste experienced:

"On arriving in my past life, I had a strong feeling of abandonment and intense sadness. It is during the civil war, and my brother and I are very close. He goes off to the war and is killed. I am not at all close to my parents, so the feeling of being abandoned by my brother completely devastates me."

I took Celeste through a forgive-and-release exercise to forgive her brother for abandoning her.

"I grow up and I become a dance hall whore. This is where I meet Jerry, the man I'm dating in this life. He is a ranch hand and comes into town a lot. We end up falling in love. We're planning to get married, but I'm killed in a shooting accident."

Next, I floated her back into early childhood in this life.

"I am two years old and I have polio. My parents have to leave me at the hospital for almost a month and I'm not allowed to see them at all. This is where all the trauma comes from, as I'm not at all prepared. Everything just happens so fast—I wake up one morning and am paralyzed, so my parents had to leave me at the hospital.

"Besides my tremendous fear over not understanding my paralysis, I'm also abandoned by my parents with no explanation. In the regression, I truly relived the whole experience."

That is an understatement. Celeste just sobbed uncontrollably from a place deep inside her. In her forgive-and-release process, she was able to let her mother and father know that she now understands and that it's okay.

She later told me, "I don't have that anger anymore or that feeling of abandonment. And I don't get those horrible panic attacks anymore."

I then took her forward into the future, where she saw her daughter married and happy. She also saw herself very happy, too, and much thinner! "It was so strange, because I saw myself thinner and very, very happy. I also saw myself with someone who is very well off, something to do with a huge ranch."

Next, a spirit showed up for her. From my description, Celeste told me, "That sounds like my paternal grandfather. I was very close to him, but when I was two, just before the polio, he was murdered."

"You've been his child in another life but this time around, you came back too late to be his child, so you chose him as your grandfather."

"It makes sense that I was close to him and yet I lost him," she said ruefully. "That abandonment thing again."

30. Maria

Maria and I worked in the evenings together years ago in my toy party plan business. One night, we were sitting in my office talking and it suddenly got very cold. We were freezing. "Someone's here," I said. "It's a man, standing beside you with his hand on your shoulder."

I described him, and Maria shouted, "That's father. He passed away years and years ago. I didn't know you were psychic!"

I smiled, and Maria said. "That's odd. I suddenly got very, very warm. And I can feel his hand on my shoulder."

"He wants me to tell you that life on the other side is wonderful and that he's around each of you in the family to guide you, protect you and be there for you. He's saying that he's helping you with the problems you're having with your husband. He also says that you will have two children."

"I'm confused," Maria said. "I've had two miscarriages with my present husband and two with my first husband. The doctors say that with my history of problems, I probably won't have any children."

Puzzled, we let it go, but about six years later, Maria told me, "I kept asking myself, how could I be a mother? But what my father predicted came true. You see, Pablo, my husband, had two children in another country. Well, those two children have come to live with us. And even though Pablo has now passed away, my stepchildren are my own. So, I definitely am the mother of two children."

Once, well before Pablo had crossed, Maria had come for a reading and I described a man, alive and well, in her energy.

"That's Dan," she said.

"He is married but very much in love with you," I said. "And you love him," I added.

"He was divorced and we met and fell in love, but he ended up going back to his wife and children. I was heart-broken, but we continued to see each other until I got remarried. When my husband died, Dan started calling me again to make sure I was okay. We're talking seventeen years later, and all of a sudden we rekindled our love and our affair."

"You two have been together in a previous life and were extremely close, as one spirit. You decided that in this life, you would not be together because you had to grow as individuals."

"You're right about us, but it's been impossible for me to stay away from him these last three years since my husband died. I guess it's because we carried so much love over from that past life that it's hard to let go."

"I'm seeing that he'll never leave his wife even though he says he has a bad marriage."

"I think you're wrong because of the way he talks about his wife to me," Maria protested.

"Why not have a regression to discover your past ties with your husband and to see how the puzzle pieces fit together?" I asked Maria.

"My husband in this life is from Peru," she replied. "So much about him was so different from anyone I've ever known." She agreed to the regression, and this is what she found.

"I am back in the Inca civilization, and Pablo, my husband, is my son. I can see him so well, his face, what he looks like as a baby and as a child. He has the same mannerisms back then that he had when we were married. I love being his Mom in that lifetime. He is so wonderful, so darling. And then he dies at the age of twelve."

Afterwards, Maria explained, "Seeing that he had been my son makes sense. It explains our relationship in this life a lot more, for I was more like a mother to him in this life also. We did not have a passionate relationship, but we definitely had a bonding of sorts. I felt that I was a catalyst to help him learn to survive here in the United States, more the mother, the caretaker. The love was there but it was so different. He would cuddle me, hold me, hug me, but more like a son around his mama. It didn't make sense to me at the time, but that was okay. The regression helped me understand him more because, even though there were things about him I didn't like (he had a couple of mistresses while we were married) yet I tolerated it but wondered why I did. The regression told me it was because I was the Mama, and you always love your son, no matter what."

Next, I took Maria forward two years in her current lifetime. She told me, "I'm alone, he is gone."

"How did he die?" I asked, shocked that she'd been shown her husband's death.

"Heart attack," Maria answered. "You know, that amazed me because I never thought of him as being a heart attack candidate. So I knew that thought didn't come from my conscious mind. He was forty nine when I did the regression."

"Maria, I'm upset that you witnessed his death," I confessed. "I instructed your Higher Self to show you only what is right and good for you to know."

"But, it was good for me to know. Being pre-warned will take away the heavy trauma for me when his death takes place."

Pablo's fatal heart attack occurred four months later, and Maria told me, "Thank goodness I attended your classes and learned that spirits can easily make their presence known. Only about a month after he died, the phone rang as I was blow-drying my hair. I turned off the dryer and went to the phone. During the call, the blow dryer turned on. I figured that maybe it slipped and the 'on' button had been hit. However, the dryer was exactly where I'd left it, but the 'on' button was pressed down. While I was standing there, I saw the 'on' button turn 'off' before my very eyes.

"I said, 'Pablo, knock it off, okay!'

"One night, the lights started going on and off. When I told

Pablo to stop, he did. That same night, he went to a friend's home and turned her television on and off. One day, in front of me and Gigi, his daughter, he tried to pull a tissue out of the box."

"Much of this is because he doesn't realize he's died. He just can't accept it," I said.

Comments on Maria

With regressions, the puzzle pieces always fit together. Knowing Maria's relationship with her husband, Pablo, I wasn't surprised to see that she was his mom in a past life. We are the sum total of all our past lives, and as a past mom and son, there was a tremendous bond, a protective feeling, so it made sense that their sexual life in this life wasn't strong.

Notice that Pablo had a sudden death. Once again, when we die suddenly, we are not prepared mentally for the transition, so he remained earthbound. That is when we—family and friends— need to keep telling our loved ones, "Go to the Light."

There is nothing "magical" about what I do. Anyone can learn to "tune into" your higher self, or God within, to spirit guides, or to family and friends who have crossed over. The hardest part is learning to trust, because it always feels as though the thoughts are just your own. That trust comes with practice.

Maria certainly trusted what she got from Pablo—it's hard to dismiss it when physical objects are moving around and the lights are going on and off!

◆ ◆ ◆

Many clients ask me what they can do to make things go more smoothly in their lives. I always tell them the same things:

Keep a picture in your mind that the future is positive and that it will be better than anything you have ever known. Appreciate all that you have. Focus on what is working in your life and it will increase.

Focus on bringing out the good in people by recognizing what is good and beautiful about them. Overlook their faults and weaknesses. Speak to them of what you love and appreciate about them. If you do, you will find problems between you beginning to resolve themselves, even if you haven't worked directly on finding solutions.

In a difficult relationship, imagine that, in some way, this person is bringing you many blessings and good things. You will find the energy between you becoming more beautiful and you will become a more perfect light.

When experiencing a painful situation, decide that you will grow with joy rather than through struggle or pain. Realize that this situation is offering you opportunities to grow stronger and more whole within. The ability to see all situations, people, and events from this positive perspective will help you to rise out of the denser levels of energy and up onto your spiritual pathway.

Love and accept who you are, not who you will be or should be.

Think of at least one soul quality—patience, love, forgiveness, humility, or compassion, for example—that you are more able to express since you drew a troublesome situation to you. Send your love and forgiveness to everyone involved. And remember to have love and forgive for yourself for having created this challenging growth opportunity!

31. Carly

Curiosity brought Carly to see me. For many years, I had been a client at the beauty salon where she worked, and after learning that I did spiritual readings, she really wanted to see what spirits I would see around her. She found great comfort from learning that family and friends who die are still with us or around us most of the time.

Carly's initial nervousness when the reading began quickly turned to fascination as I described the spirits in her life, some who

139

had died and some still alive and part of her life. I began by describing two of her daughters who had some messages for her. Then Carly asked, "Can you see my middle daughter?"

Much to Carly's amazement, I found my body twisting and contorting before her eyes.

"Megan is retarded," Carly explained, "and her body shape is very stiff and curled. I'm amazed."

"Megan's Higher Self is here," I told her. "She wants you to know that she and you agreed, on a higher level, to her returning to finish what she needed to do. She wants to teach others to be more compassionate and understanding of the handicapped."

I found myself crying uncontrollably as I picked up on Megan's feelings of joy at being able to contact her mother through me.

A few months later, Carly returned for another reading and her first regression. Before the regression got underway, Carly told me, "I carry so much fear. Many times when my other girls are out alone or with friends, this horrible fear of losing them comes over me."

I asked Carly's higher self to take her back to the relevant lifetime. "Well, I'm in a lifetime where the three of us are sisters. We are in a fiery car crash and I see the two of them burn to death."

Carly cried her eyes out while in her altered state of consciousness. Then I led her in a release process while still in that altered state. She is now completely free of the fear that something bad will happen to her daughters.

In another session with Carly, I was helping her with a circulation problem in her feet. As I worked on her, I suddenly saw the Blessed Mother standing beside her saying, "This is my child. She is Jacinta from Fatima."

When I told Carly, she started sobbing—some deep part of her knew this to be true. I loaned her a book about Our Lady of Fatima, and from the pictures of the three children of Fatima, Carly noticed a strong resemblance between Jacinta and her appearance today.

While reading the book, she felt an overwhelming sadness and told me, "As a child in this life, I said the rosary a lot. And that was one of the many messages given to the children at Fatima."

In another reading, I saw and described a man in Carly's life. She replied, "I have deep feelings for him but, because I'm married to Bob, I've never acted on them."

I observed, "I can see that although you have a good husband, you're not happy in your marriage."

"The problem is that I feel nothing sexually, nothing emotionally. It's just like living with a wall—very cold, very, very cold."

"Maybe we should go into a regression to find the source of your feelings for Bob since you don't know what the problem is on the conscious level."

That regression unearthed some disturbing information: "I'm in the deep, sick depression I've been used to feeling so much in my life. At these times, I don't like myself or anyone else around me."

"Let's go back to the source where you first had this feeling," I suggested.

"I'm in the covered wagon days and my father then is my husband now. In that lifetime, he is a very big, burly man, very evil, very wicked looking, cruel and abusive. I'm thirteen when he brutally rapes me and I become pregnant. He molests me constantly. I'm crying uncontrollably and screaming how much I hate him and want him dead.

"I'm the middle child of three. The oldest child is my oldest daughter in this life but she's my older brother in that past life. He's kind of my protector against my father. I have a younger brother, who's my younger brother in this life, too. When my older brother tries to protect me from my father, dad beats him. My father is killed when he falls off a horse and hits his head. It was such a relief!"

As always, the puzzle pieces did fit together! No wonder Carly had no emotions toward, and was cold to, her current husband to the point of being unable to stand even the thought of him touching her.

At a later time, we were doing another regression to probe Carly's emotional connection with her husband. She was feeling that it was time to leave her family and move on, but she felt an overwhelming sadness at the thought of leaving them. I put her into an altered state and got her in touch with her feeling of "void." She started crying and I saw that this feeling was connected with the life at Fatima. I took her back into that life when she was the small child, Jacinta, who had died young. She began to cry really hard and said, "I did not want to leave my family."

In Carly's words: "We put little Jacinta in a balloon and I saw myself in that balloon, too. I told Jacinta that I loved her and said goodbye. Then I stepped out of the balloon and let it go. Afterwards, I felt light-hearted and clear in my feelings!"

Carly requested another regression to explore a past life with her father. She wanted to understand the feelings she has for him today. Here's what she found.

"I am a five-year-old boy. I live in the barn and it is very cold. I am alone since my family died when I was three. They—mom, dad, and my sister—are killed by soldiers. I am hiding so that no one finds me. Two weeks after my family dies, I am wandering around. A family takes me in, they are kind. The father of that family is my dad in this life. I am now four years old and he is good to me. He is happy to have me. His wife in that life is no one I know. They have a daughter who resents me being there and is jealous of me.

"I am now six and am in the barn again. The father is rude, pushy and angry. He is unhappy with himself. I am numb. I have no feelings, I am cold, so cold. I don't know why I'm in the barn. I didn't do anything wrong, nobody wants me."

"Go into the mother's feelings," I suggested.

"The mother is jealous because I brought happiness to her

husband which she doesn't know how to handle. And she doesn't appreciate my closeness with her husband. The daughter hates me because I take some of her Dad's attention and time away from her. She wants to hurt me."

"We are going ahead one more year."

"I leave the barn and the family, and go into the city. Another family takes me in, and they are very loving and caring. That husband and wife are my uncle and aunt in this life."

"We are now going ahead five years, to when you are twelve."

"I am in school and I'm very happy."

"We will now go to your marriage in that life."

"I have been married for ten years and am very happy. We have four children together and live a good life. I die at age fifty-three of a sudden heart attack, leaving my wife and children. She is a very strong woman but she is very, very sad."

"I feel that your dad in that life (the man with the barn) likes you very much but his daughter and wife adversely swayed him. You saw him as a very weak man and you hated him for it. You knew that he could have brought you warm blankets and clothing but he was weak. So, in today's life, you get very upset when you see him drinking because you're reliving another weakness with him. In many ways, he has let you down again."

"Doing a forgive-and-release process with him in the past life, when he was too weak to save you from the cold barn, will help you to tolerate his weakness with alcohol in this life."

"It has already!"

Comments on Carly

Carly's regressions give you concrete examples of how, when you go to "the source" of a problem and go through a forgive-and-release process, the problem almost always simply dissolves, especially when the source of the problem is from a past life. It's much easier to forgive someone for something they did in a past life than it is with someone who wronged you in this life.

The important thing to always remember is that you don't have to condone, you need to forgive.

Carly's handicapped daughter, Megan, is a highly evolved old soul. When someone is physically and mentally handicapped, it teaches the rest of us not to be judgmental. Everyone in a family grows from this difficult type of situation. Megan has since crossed over and is now unencumbered by her physical body. She's free at last!

As a footnote to this story, about a month after she crossed over in 1996, someone who used to work for her father was at the cemetery to visit the graves of his mother and grandmother. It was deserted and he was alone. Out of nowhere, a girl appeared wearing a long, white, flowing robe with a hood. She handed him a palm leaf and said, "Give this to Bob!"

"Bob who?" he asked.

She said, "The man you used to work for."

With that, she simply disappeared. It was six years ago that he'd worked for Bob and didn't even know that Megan had crossed!

32. Janice

Janice came to see me at the suggestion of her husband. She had just lost her father and was struggling with some internal conflicts. She came in with a somewhat confrontational attitude, like, "Okay, show me what you can do."

A man showed up who said to Janice, "I am very happy to see you."

I described him as a man in his middle fifties, about five-ten, sandy blond hair with a bald spot on the top of his head, and blue eyes. "He has a message for you. He's saying he wishes that he had told you he loved you more!"

This scored a few points with Janice, since her father had indeed been five-ten when he died aged 52, and had a bald spot on the top of his head and blue eyes. She told me, "From the time I was thirteen, he had stopped telling me he loved me because it seemed we were always in some sort of battle, especially through my teenage years. He would always tell my mother he loved me but he would never tell me. We always argued about it. This continued into young adulthood. I knew he loved me, but I needed to hear it. About the best time that my father and I had were the two years when he was dying. I have no doubt it's my father you're speaking to. Can you ask him why he died?"

"He says that it was his time to die. Everything happened exactly as it was supposed to."

"But, at the time of his death, he was very angry about dying so young with liver cancer. One of the last things he ever said to me was, 'I'm afraid that if I ever take any pain medication, I'm never going to wake up.'

"When he was admitted into the hospital at the end, he went into renal failure. He was crying and very uncomfortable with all the pain, and I said, 'Daddy, I'm going to get you some pain medication.'

"He said again, 'I'm afraid if I take pain medication, I'm never going to wake up.'

"I said, 'Daddy, you need the relief it will give you.' So I got the nurse and she administered some pain medicine to him. Five doses later, he was dead. So I'm having a little bit of conflict over that. Should I have respected his wishes and not gotten him the pain medication, or pushed for it?"

Of course, I knew nothing about this, so Janice found great comfort and healing from his message that everything had happened the way it was supposed to. As the session continued, he said, "Because I had been so frightened of crossing over, I'm currently helping other people cross over."

"That's certainly true. He was terrified of death," Janice confirmed.

Her father continued, "You know, I've come to like your husband."

Janice replied, "That's weird because you always thought Stan was kind of a kook and you never really understood him."

He closed the reading with, "If you ever need me, just mentally ask for me and trust that your first thoughts or the first voice to come up in your head will be me."

Today, Janice routinely talks with her dad during meditation. She finds that his answer comes to her before she even has the question out of her mind! She is also fascinated how, in regressions, she can follow the threads from one life to another. She once told me, "My favorite past life is the one where I healed animals. I never got married in that life because everyone thought I was too weird. I feel a real connection to that life and will be doing natural (holistic) healing in this life. Being regressed and actually reliving my past lives has really brought me a lot of comfort. Now, any time I think about it, I can go back to that lifetime and almost tell you exactly what I did day to day."

In a later session, I said to Janice, "I'm seeing you with a new guide—an Indian!"

"Wow. I'm really getting into the rituals of different tribes. I've been drawn to read a lot about the Indian way of life. And tomorrow, I'm going to an old Indian ruin to meditate," Janice said excitedly.

"The new guide is here to teach you. You and he have been married in several past lives."

"Isn't it interesting how different spirit guides pop in at different times," Janice said. "And, you knew nothing of my new interest in rituals, or of my upcoming trip."

"Yes, it's great how everything dovetails in. Again, the puzzle pieces fit together."

"Yes. I've sent quite a few clients to you in the past and it's interesting to watch their evolution when it comes to understanding their own spiritual path. We've all learned from you to understand how to access our guides, understand what's our own garbage and what's garbage from a past life that we're still carrying around with us now. And how to tell if we have another spirit living vicariously through us. It's fun watching us just getting to the root of our stuff, the stuff we all want to get rid of. And it's fascinating to see how it all ties together."

Comments on Janice

Our guides do change, as they did with Janice when her Indian guide joined her. Again, it was no coincidence that he joined her just before she was going to explore an old Indian ruin, and was getting into the rituals of various Indian tribes. In fact, I feel he came first, and led her to an interest in Indian matters.

33. Monique

I'd given readings for Monique before, and she came to me just after starting a new job with a national rehab company. Unbeknown to me, she and her co-workers had discovered something startling about themselves.

Monique handed me a group photograph and casually asked, "What do you think about a couple of these people that I met in training? We all met in Salem for our new-hire orientation.

She was blown away when I said, "This sounds kind of funny, but you were all passengers together on the Mayflower and you made a pact that you would come back and meet once every however many years. Does this sound right to you? Remember, no one can tell you about a past life without you feeling that it's definitely possible."

Monique said, "It sounds right on to me because that's how the entire group felt. We spent two weeks together. These people came from all over the country—Wisconsin, Illinois, Boston, Arkansas, Oregon, and Oklahoma. Out of about sixty people total, thirteen of us had separate accommodation from the rest of the group. The rest had rooms in a beautiful hotel, and we had two apartments and a condo, away from town.

"The first night we were together, we all went out to dinner and it was like we'd known each other for years. We were fast friends immediately. We laughed all night long. It was a very warm feeling. On the last day, we all cried and took group pictures. It's odd, but we simply didn't interact with the others. We did things like walk through the cemeteries where actual passengers on the Mayflower were buried."

"So, did you all actually think you had been on the Mayflower together?" I asked.

"Yes. We took a picture of all of us standing next to a big old rock by the ocean in Salem. Someone referred to us as pilgrims. It's so uncanny that every one of us felt it, even the people who didn't believe in reincarnation. It was all we could talk about. We didn't talk about it as a group initially, just one-on-one, because some people were embarrassed about it. But finally it came out in the open, and I'm so glad that you confirmed it without knowing anything about it."

Monique then changed the subject. "My Dad passed over in 1978. It was such a special feeling in my first reading when you described him, you said, "You'll feel his hand on your back and neck. It will be a warm feeling. You know, I felt it! I think my first reading, I sobbed the entire time. It's such a good feeling to know you can communicate with a loved one after losing them."

"It's also good for them because they feel great that they can communicate with us," I added.

"Whenever someone in my family passes away and I have a reading, they always come through first. It's such an emotional experience. Dad said things through you about my career, my brother, my Mom, the family relationship—things that you would have no way of knowing."

Then Monique reminded me of a humorous incident. "Do you remember when my grandmother came through? She's my mother's mother, and she and my father never got along. When she came through and my Dad was already there, she just barreled right through him. You described this pushy lady who 'barged her way through' saying that she had no time for him and was going to be the first to talk to me. Well, that's exactly how she is in daily life. That's exactly how she treated my poor dad. In the reading, he allowed her to go first, which is what he did in real life."

In a later reading, Monique started by saying, "My mother and I don't have the best relationship in the world."

"Yes, I can see that you play a sort of 'one-upmanship' thing in your relationship. That's because in a past life, you were sisters, and your grandmother—your mother's mother—was your mother. You were always the favorite daughter, and she would constantly say to your sister/mother, 'Why can't you be more like your sister?' 'Can't you do this better?' 'You're not as good, you're not as pretty.'

"The two of you have carried that rivalry over into this life," I explained.

"Oh, that helps me understand her better. So it's not just a 'here and now' thing."

"Yes. It's not just because of what happened last week or last year. It's because of what happened in a past life that you need to resolve."

"But even knowing that, it's still hard."

Comments on Monique

With Monique and her mom, it's fun to see how the pieces fit together, how our lives are interwoven from one lifetime to the next. But as Monique said, "It's still hard."

It truly does help, however, in understanding some of our relationships. You may not necessarily like some of the people in your life, but at least you can understand them and why they are in your life. It's important to remember that what you experience in your daily life—the challenges, emotions and relationships—are the very things your higher self put there to learn from.

34. Jill

Jill had no inkling that another spirit was enjoying life through her. In one of my seminars, I was talking about how many souls walk the halls of the hospitals and cemeteries looking for a living "host." I "randomly" chose Jill for an example and said, "Let's say that Jill picked someone up while in the hospital having her baby."

Suddenly, everyone in the room was startled to hear a very loud click. They all said, "That's weird," and laughed nervously among themselves.

Then I started leading the group through the clearing. I said something like, "You are in Jill's body and your name is Phyllis." (The name Phyllis came to me immediately.)

There are no accidents or coincidences, and I saw that Phyllis had been in the hospital having a baby and died in childbirth. She'd jumped into Jill because she had longed to hold and love the child that she would never have. Having just given birth, Jill was very open and this gave Phyllis her chance.

I told her to go into the light, and that friends and family would be there to meet her. Jill later told the group, "She thanked me for the opportunity to hold and love a child. Then she stepped out of my body and I saw her 'shoot' into the light very quickly. Once she'd gone, my body tingled and was very hot. I also felt very light headed and emotional."

As Jill shared her experience with the class, she started sobbing intensely—a combination of sorrow for Phyllis who'd never had a chance to hold and love her own baby, and joy that she'd found the light and walked into it.

Jill later told me, "At first, I couldn't believe that something like this could happen to me. But the next day, I felt incredibly light-hearted, like the first time you fall in love. I had a little extra spring in my feet, also. I guess I felt more like myself, when all along I was thinking that my depression was because of the 'baby blues'."

Comments on Jill

When the loud 'click' happened after I 'randomly' picked Jill to use as an example, that was spirit's way of confirming what I was saying. Jill really had picked up a spirit while at the hospital delivering her second daughter. Coincidence that I chose Jill? Or that I picked the name Phyllis? Of course not!

When my children were younger, after their Dad crossed over, we would often linger at the dinner table together talking. When I was talking, a loud 'click' right above the table would signal that their Dad was agreeing with me. The girls would look up and say, "Okay, okay, Dad, we're listening!"

We all need to go to the hospital from time to time, either as a patient or a visitor. It's very easy to protect your energies from unwanted discarnate intruders. I simply visualize a beautiful, white, iridescent bubble around myself and call it, "God's protective white light." I put this around myself every morning before I get out of bed. I'll often add visualizing a fire coming up and around my light bubble, but not touching it, and say, "All negativity will burn off before it gets to me."

When I'm around negative people, I visualize them in a gold bubble and I mentally say, "All of their negativity will neutralize before it gets out of them."

This renders you transparent to their negative energies and keeps discarnate souls from merging with you.

35. Anna

Anna came to see me when things between her and her husband continued to deteriorate. She had heard about me from a friend and made an appointment for a reading.

As soon as Anna walked in, I immediately picked up on all her problems. "I see that you were devastated by the recent death of your mother. You and your husband are having major problems and it looks like you're seeing someone else. I can see how much you love this other man. Is your son his?"

Anna nodded sheepishly.

"He cares a great deal about you, but due to money concerns, he won't leave his wife."

The words simply tumbled out of Anna. "I feel so much better just talking to someone else about the situation who isn't judgmental but is just here to help. Having an affair with a married man isn't something I'm proud of or want anybody to know. I don't like lying to so many people for so many years."

After the reading, Anna brought me up to speed on her story:

"I thought that I was a happily married woman, never thinking about anyone else except my husband and our one daughter. We had our problems like any other married couple, but nothing that I thought was major.

"However, in June, 1974, I met Stan who worked at the same company. The first time I laid eyes on him, there was an intense physical attraction. He was so nice-looking, sweet, kind and a great personality. We had so much in common and began talking. I learned that he was also married and had one child. Within a few days, we had become close friends. About two months later, my husband started to freak out. He was very good at putting me down, letting me know how stupid I was, how unattractive, what a poor mother, and so on. But now, the verbal abuse starting getting worse towards my daughter and myself. My self-esteem was the pits, so when Stan started to show me attention, I really ate it up. He made me laugh and made me feel like I was the most beautiful woman in the world.

"For at least five months, we just stayed friends and never even went out to lunch. We would just say 'Hi' in the morning before work, and he would stop by my work area just to talk. Finally, we started going out to lunch. The two things we sort of agreed not to talk about were each other's home life and how we felt about each other.

"About a year after we met, over lunch Stan said, 'There's something I need to talk to you about, something personal, and I'm not sure how you'll take it.'

" 'Stan, we're friends,' I said. 'You can tell me anything.'

" 'Okay,' he blurted out, 'I'm very attracted to you and would like to be more than just friends.'

"Well, I was shocked, but I have to be honest, it really made me feel good that this great looking guy was attracted to me. I just sat there not knowing what to say. Then I said, 'But we're both married and I don't want to hurt anyone.'

"He didn't say anything, so I asked him, 'What do you have in mind?'

"I wasn't interested in just a physical relationship at this time in my life, so on the way back to work, we both agreed to just think about it for a week and then talk about how we felt. I was a nervous wreck that whole week. I was so confused. I was unhappy at home, but I was brought up not to cheat on my husband, especially with a married man. A lot of people could get hurt. We both had kids to think about.

"When we met that next week for lunch, I told him, 'I don't think it would be a good idea and I think we should just stay friends.'

"He felt the same and we continued to just be friends. A couple of months later, we were both invited to a work party on New Year's Eve. Both Stan's wife and my husband were at the party, too. When my husband and I arrived, Stan and his wife were the first people I saw. He looked fabulous and I noticed that his wife was very attractive.

"Stan came right over, took my hand and said, 'You look beautiful.'

"I introduced him to my husband, and Stan introduced us to his wife. All night, Stan and I couldn't keep our eyes off each other. Around 11:30, he came over to ask my husband if he would mind us dancing together. 'No, go ahead and enjoy yourselves.'

"When we got to the dance floor, it happened to be a slow dance and I melted in his arms. I couldn't believe that I could feel this way about anyone. I was so nervous because I knew that everyone in the room knew how attracted we were to each other. It was very hard not to just tilt my head up and give him a kiss. When midnight struck, everyone was kissing everyone and, to my surprise, Stan came over and gave me the sweetest kiss, not too long, but I definitely got the message.

"For the next few weeks, all I could think about was that kiss and how much I wanted to be with him. I felt guilty but couldn't help myself. So when Stan asked if I would meet him for dinner over the weekend, I agreed. That's when the lies began. After four dinner dates, we started a physical relationship. It was unbelievable, like a dream come true. It took no time at all for me to fall in love with him. He was very cautious what he said to me, though. He would tell me that he cared about me, but never did he tell me that he loved me or that he would ever leave his wife. But deep down, I would tell myself he did love me and I always thought that someday we would be together.

"We continued to see each other for at least two years when I found out I was pregnant. I was pretty sure that it was his since I hardly ever had sex with my husband. When I told Stan, the first thing he asked was, 'Is it mine?'

" 'I'm almost certain it is,' I replied.

" 'What do you want from me?' he asked.

"I said, 'Nothing really. I'll raise the child. With both of us married to other people, what good would it do to make a disaster out of everyone's lives?'

"Throughout my pregnancy he was very supportive and offered to help me with whatever I needed. He visited me and the baby in the hospital, but after that he never asked about my son. Whenever I talked about him, he got very nervous and would be quiet.

"When my son was about eighteen months old, we started up a physical relationship again. I had missed him so much and wanted to be with him. He helped me through some real rough times, but I always wanted much more of him than he was willing to give. I used to just sit by the phone waiting for him to call. He would never give me much warning, but I would jump at his beck and call. I told myself, if I show him how good I am for him, and how much I love him, then he'll fall in love with me, leave his wife and we'll get married.

"About three years later, I found out that Stan was also was seeing someone else in addition to me and his wife. When I confronted him, he confessed. The shock made me very ill for several months. I was so depressed. What a fool I'd been. I always believed deep down that Stan loved me and that the only reason he was not with me was because of his two children and the expense of divorce and child support. What a joke. I couldn't believe that I was that stupid and naive. He just wanted to be with different women all the time.

"I stopped seeing him and refused to take his calls. I kept putting God's white light around me and asking for guidance to get him out of my life. But no matter how much I tried to cut him out of my life, I kept making excuses for him and finally talked to him on the phone.

"Even though I know he is scum, I still love him very much. But over the years, I think I've outgrown Stan. We're in completely different places in our lives and do not want the same things. I know I need to work on forgiving him and letting him go. Daily, I ask my guides to bring the right person in my life who will love me and my children as much as I loved Stan.

"Your seminars and readings have shown me that I deserve to have a good man in my life. It hasn't been easy, though. About a year after starting the classes, the abuse from my husband became physical again, but the spiritual growth had made me strong enough to leave him and I filed for a divorce.

"I thank God I had you to help me through the ordeal. My husband fought me all the way and our divorce took almost two years to become final. He was trying to get my children away from me and to turn all our family and friends against me. He even tried to get me fired from my job.

"You kept telling me that it would work out, but during those two years of fighting, it was hard to see the light at the end of the tunnel. You were right; divorce was the best thing I ever did for me and my kids. My ex had become physically abusive to my daughter and would hit her for no reason, putting her down the same way he did me.

"Now both children are doing fantastically and I'm not worried about him coming home from work one day and killing us all. I continued to see Stan during all this time, but not as frequently as in the past, in case my husband found out. He would surely have killed both of us."

Comments on Anna

Know that you are already complete, already whole, and that nothing external to yourself in the physical world can make you any more complete. Too often, we look to relationships to find happiness. Instead, first find happiness within, then the right relationship will follow.

Work with doing affirmations on your self-worth while looking yourself in the eyes in a mirror, affirmations like: *Love is everywhere, I am loving and lovable...I deserve an honest, faithful, monogamous, loving relationship and I accept it now...I am perfect, whole and complete...All my relationships are harmonious...I am now opening my consciousness to a relationship that's best for my highest good...I am willing to release the pattern within me that is creating this relationship problem...I am willing to release the need for uncomfortable relationships...I am releasing my fear of being alone...I love and approve of myself exactly as I am...I experience love wherever I go.*

We all need to remove the floppy disks from our heads that have been programmed since birth, insert a blank floppy disk, and program it with affirmations on self-esteem and love. Our subconscious mind can easily be reprogrammed. Remember the saying, "Garbage in, garbage out." Work on your desires daily through visualization and affirmations.

Buddhism teaches, "Never is hate diminished by hate. It is only diminished by love." This is an eternal law. Love and hate can switch places rapidly when we're having relationship problems. Don't force yourself to make a relationship work. It can't be forced. Know when it's time to gently send the other person love and move on.

When there is a breakup or problems in a relationship, one partner is usually devastated and goes through an overwhelming sadness. Know that if it's your partner's divine time to move on, it is also your time to move on. Allow yourself grieving time, then move on physically, mentally and spiritually.

Allow everyone's imperfections to be: "I allow you to be who you want to be, but I'm angry and above your actions. I don't deserve your actions so we are no longer lovers or partners."

When there is a betrayal in a relationship, it's nearly impossible to ever trust that person again. Love and trust go hand-in-hand. Send him or her your God light and move on. You can't change someone else, but you can change yourself. When a betrayal happens, deal with the pain and then get in a quiet, meditative place and ask your angels, your guides, your higher self to give you "the bigger picture".

Almost invariably, you'll realize that your betrayer just did you the biggest favor he or she could have done for you. You had become comfortable in your rut, but you weren't happy. If one partner isn't happy, neither is the other.

In Anna's case, her lover of 22 years was a catalyst for her. He gave her the courage, the strength to move on, to leave an abusive relationship. Even if you're still living with someone who has betrayed you but the timing isn't right for you to move on, the bigger picture may show you that you're trying to fix something that's not fixable. So start doing things and going places that make you happy.

Are there people to whom you are sending a lot of energy but who aren't growing, or who feel like burdens to you in some way? Turn these people over to their own higher selves to help them grow. Send them God light, and release your responsibility for making their lives work. Some of you will know you are carrying people because you have shoulder and back problems. If people feel like burdens, it is a sign that "carrying" them is not for their higher good. You may be taking away their lessons and slowing down their growth. They may become dependent on you and stop taking responsibility for making their own lives work. You are, in essence, an "enabler" when you let them drain you of your energies.

We all draw lessons to us from which to grow. We can either use these lessons as stumbling blocks or stepping-stones. Once you acknowledge that you write your life script and hand it out to your loved ones so that you can grow spiritually, then it's impossible to stay in the "victim" role. Know that whatever happens does so for a reason. Figure out the reason, then move on.

The forgive-and-release process enters into this situation very strongly. Without condoning what the other has done, you need to have your higher self, or God within, forgive their higher self or God within. This way you're not dealing with the personalities involved that hurt you.

Anna needs to forgive herself for having an affair. Once she does, she won't draw men to her who are unfaithful. This will also free her up to magnetize into her life her true soul mate. Like attracts like, so vibrate at the same frequency as whatever you want in a relationship.

Until we do the forgive-and-release process, we walk around with an "unavailable" sign on our forehead, so we won't be magnetizing in the person who is on our level, our soul-mate or twin flame.

When trying to draw in your soul mate, don't assume you know who it is. Every morning say, "Heavenly Father (or Spirit, or whatever), I'm putting my long term relationship in your hands, thy will be done. Have happen what's best for my highest good."

"Thy will be done" is such an old-fashioned term but it means so much. God didn't say that some of us could have a loving honest, faithful, monogamous relationship and some couldn't. We all came to earth to grow spiritually, but it's almost impossible to grow spiritually if we're in a miserable, dishonest relationship.

"Have happen what's best for my highest good" is also very powerful. It's for our highest good to draw in someone who's on a similar spiritual path. It's for our highest good to draw in our soul mate.

We can love someone deeply, but that doesn't mean we have to put up with his or her shenanigans, live with them or put our lives on hold for them. We need to get out of the victim role and move on.

36. Amy

Amy had been to me for a few readings, so when she had the following experience, she immediately phoned me. Her family has lived in the house they're in now for over a hundred years. She and her husband have been renovating for the last few years, and were putting in a new bathroom. When they opened up the ceiling, a feeling of "electricity" ran through the entire room.

Upon entering the room, I felt very strong energy present. I walked into the space where the bathroom was being built and saw that, many years ago, a porch used to be in the exact same place. I saw an older couple sitting on a wooden swing on the porch and described them to Amy.

Amy checked the original floor plan of the house and sure enough, a porch once occupied that exact spot. The date on the plan told Amy that the couple was her great-great-grandparents. She produced a photo of them for me and they looked exactly as I saw them! Satisfied that they were "friendly ghosts," Amy continued with the renovations.

Comments on Amy

Amy's description of the feeling of "electricity running through the whole room" was very accurate and typical.

Culturally, the level of spiritual awareness is growing rapidly. It's not that unusual anymore to hear people talk about reincarnation who would once have scoffed at the idea. As more people sense the presence of a loved one who has crossed over, the level of consciousness is truly rising and people are finally recognizing their own powers within.

37. Darin and Vivian

Vivian had been to me for several readings, and when she called to book a reading, I immediately saw the problem.

"How are you doing?" I asked.

"Things aren't going well."

"It's concerning a problem with alcohol, isn't it?" I asked.

"Yes, it's my fiancé's drinking problem."

At the reading, the first spirit I described for her was that of her fiancé, Darin. I told her, "I'm seeing that his father died an alcoholic and at the moment of death, his spirit "jumped" into Darin, who was only twelve at the time."

"That's exactly the age Darin was when he started drinking," a surprised Vivian said. "He's now thirty-one. His drinking is a real problem between us. Because of it, I'm worried about whether things will work out between us, and whether we should move in together as we planned."

"Will Darin come in for a clearing?" I asked.

"Yes, I'm sure he will because he wants our relationship to last."

During Darin's clearing, he felt his face contorting, and he felt a definite physical sensation when his father left his body. He also experienced a feeling of deep sadness. His desire to drink also left during the clearing.

"It's important for you not to think of your father for at least three days because that could easily pull him back in if he isn't fully in the light yet. I can get the spirit out but your drinking is now such a habit thanks to your dad merging with you that you need to work on ridding yourself of that habit even after the clearing."

Vivian later told me, "I really feel that his father is gone. Darin didn't even want a drink for maybe three weeks, which is a record for him. He is drinking again, but he's not mean when he drinks, as he was before. His father would become mean when drinking."

Comments on Vivian and Darin

Someone who does just clearings for a living went to many AA meetings and told me that he'd found as many as 26 spirits drinking through one alcoholic! It's appalling to realize how many discarnate souls stay on the earth plane, just waiting to find the right person to possess. So, whenever you feel earthbound spirits around you, tell them firmly to go to the light!

Those who have any destructive habits when they die take their habits to the other side with them. Whether it be smoking, drinking, drugs or any addictive habit, they often merge with a family member or friend to continue with their addiction. Or, if they find someone who enjoys drinking, they will possess them, and the drinker then will find his urges to drink getting stronger and stronger.

Get rid of your destructive habits before you die, or before the habit kills you. It's easier to get rid of it on this side than it is after your transition! It will definitely hold up your spiritual progression if you don't.

38. Belle

I first met Belle when she and I attended a Shirley MacLaine seminar in 1986. Participants were asked to find someone in the audience to do an exercise with, someone we did not know. Belle and I chose each other, and discovered that we lived just five miles apart.

For several months after that, Belle thought about looking me up but couldn't remember my name. One day, she was arranging for patient transportation at the American Cancer Society where she

*volunteered. She called a volunteer driver, who couldn't come in
because she was taking a seminar—with me, of all people!*

*Belle immediately called me and made an appointment. She
arrived for the reading particularly depressed with the way her life was
going.*

I told Belle, "The first spirits here are a man and a women who
are vying to be first to talk to you. They're both anxious to make
contact with you. I've never seen that happen before. The lady is
not real tall, she's chunky, she's wearing a dress, has short, dark
gray, curly hair in ringlets, as though it's permed. She had cancer
and she's pleased that you're working with the Cancer Society.
She's crying joyously over making this connection with you. Can
you feel a warmth or tingling in your shoulders? She's bending over
you and putting her hands on your shoulders."

Belle said, "That's my adoptive mother, Helen. I do feel as
though someone is touching my shoulders. My throat feels like it's
on fire, like I have something to say and can't say it. My heart is
really beating fast. Racing."

"She's very pleased with your involvement in the metaphysical
church. You're on the right track. You're around a lot of negativity,
though. Four people are giving you problems—your husband, your
stepson, your daughter and your stepdaughter. Don't let them beat
you down. You are strong. She's saying you're a very old soul and
that you are very guided, even though you are bull-headed. She's
not an earthbound spirit. She's come down from a very high plane.

"A bald-headed man is standing next to your mother. He's got
a big smile and he's got his arm around her. He has a very big heart,
and shares a very special relationship with you. You were very
special to him. Helen was quite jealous of you because he cared about
you so much. He's saying, 'I'm not one of your guides, but I'll be
with you if you call on me. I'm so proud of you.' He's standing
behind you, messing up your hair. He was the quiet one of your
two parents."

Through her tears, Belle said, "You're right, he was the quiet one. I always felt as though I was very special to him, but he never could say it. It's such a relief to finally hear it and feel it. Whenever my dad walked by me, especially if my best friend Shirley was there, he would always tousle our hair."

"There's another man here. Kind of tall, slender, eyes very piercing, light brown hair with very sharp features. He's a smoker."

"That's Don, my ex-husband."

"He had a strong influence on your life. He has bitter, hateful feelings toward you. Belle, visualize him in a gold balloon and mentally say, 'All of his negativity will neutralize before it gets out of him.' Gold neutralizes. Realize that thought is energy. Do you have any questions?"

Belle said, "Would you ask dad if he had anything to do with saving my son's life."

"He most definitely did! He's standing here beaming! I'm seeing your son running out to the waves at the beach, doing flips into the waves. At one point, he flipped when there was no wave."

"He heard a snapping sound," Belle confirmed. "I felt as though someone was looking out for him."

In November 1989, Belle came to me on a mission. "I've just recently started a search for my biological mother. Can you see anything on her?"

"Yes, I'm hearing that she's terribly nervous, very thin, and very wiry. She's currently in Denver, Colorado and I have the feeling that when you go to Denver, you will be very warmly greeted by a man whose name is Jack. I think he's your father.

"I see you definitely finding your mom but that she won't be at all receptive to meeting you because she hasn't yet told her family about you. But, I see you working around all that and eventually meeting her."

Belle later told me, "Your reading spurred me on to look for more information about my mom. Both of my adoptive parents have crossed over. I found someone in San Francisco who told me how to get the information I needed from the court. She does live in Denver, and I've phoned her several times and sent her some pictures of myself. Unfortunately, she still won't agree to meet me, as she hasn't yet gotten the courage to tell her adult children about me. However, you still see me meeting her, and I'm sure you're right.

Belle added, "Oh, and that man you saw turns out to be my uncle, my birth mother's brother. She lived with him in San Francisco before she gave birth to me. Because they were living together, I can see why you felt he was my biological dad."

In September 1992, Belle called me. "I'm going back east to my son's graduation and I just wanted your thoughts about me writing my mom a letter asking if I could stop off in Denver."

"Definitely write the letter," I told her. "She will finally see you."

A few weeks later, Belle called again. "Well, I wrote and my mom called to tell me that she was very nervous about meeting. She said, 'I understand that you need to know, but just don't expect too much. I'm such a nervous person, and when I get real nervous, I get tremors. This will be the hardest thing I've ever done, but I'll meet you at the airport.'"

Belle was elated, but she developed an extremely nervous stomach. "That's because you're picking up on her vibrations," I told her, adding, "She never let go of you, but she's still afraid that, if she tells her two daughters, they won't love her. Her husband keeps trying to reassure her that they'll be fine."

Well, they did in fact meet, and on October 20, Belle came to me for another reading. I told her, "As I go in on you with your biological mother, the song *Is That All There Is* keeps running through my mind. I feel that's how you felt when you met her."

Belle laughed. "That really sums up my whole meeting with her."

"I asked to speak to your mother, and your biological mother was the first to appear. But right behind her is your adoptive mother.

164

She's feeling a little bent out of shape. Now your adoptive father's come in and he's just delighted for you. With your biological mom, I'm feeling really light-hearted. She feels like a huge weight has been lifted off her shoulders because the source of most of her nervousness has been you. She enjoyed meeting you very much, even though she had a very difficult time showing emotion."

"That's for sure."

"Although I see her hugging you," I added.

Belle said, "Yes, she did. I've just been numb since meeting her. I expected to find someone who is just like me. I guess that must be my father, because it isn't her. I don't look at all like her."

"I don't feel her heart's ever going to really open up and accept you in fully. I feel her husband will, like he's your father, even though he's not."

"He's wonderful. Much more kind and loving than she is."

"Well, she's a very unhappy lady. I'm feeling that she didn't tell you about your biological father because she didn't want to open up another wound. I feel she was very much in love with him. You are a real love child."

"She's so fragile. She had 'fragile' written all over her. But, I would have liked to ask her why she took me home from the hospital and kept me ten days. Why didn't she just leave me at the hospital? Because I always felt that I bonded with her and never bonded with anyone else. It's a real question I have, but I never felt free to ask her. I felt that she had a shield around her."

"She's been psychically holding onto you for all these years and I feel that you've been tuned into her energies."

"Could that be why I went from this normal vibrant person to this scared to death person?"

"Absolutely."

"It was especially horrible after my daughter was born. Horrible."

"It makes sense that you were tuned into her then. You were having your first child and it was a girl. There was like an umbilical cord between you that she was unable to cut. She really did love you. Deep down, she wanted to keep you but she was like a frightened bird. She didn't know how she could make it on her own. And I feel she's never let go. That's the cause of her nervousness now, I feel that if she allowed herself, her nerves could actually calm down, but it's become a habit. It's become a part of her. But, when you find the source, often the illness or ailment will just go away. Her unhappiness stems from her own inner self. She doesn't like herself and finds it easier to point fingers at everyone else. She can't forgive herself for giving you up."

"Did my father just not want to marry her, or what. Was he already married?"

"He wasn't married but he wasn't head over heels in love with her, as she was with him. I don't feel that he knew about the pregnancy. Is that true? Do you know?"

"The non-identifying papers I got said that he did but wouldn't help. But when I met her, she said that a lot of that information was incorrect."

"I really feel he didn't know."

"Can you get if she knows his name?" Belle asked.

"Yes, she does."

"Why won't she tell me?"

"Because she doesn't want to open old wounds. This was not a one-night stand! It was a real hurtful situation for her. Her brother could give you his name."

"I asked her if he could and she said definitely not. Her brother's name is John."

"I know John knows, but she may try to cut off communications with you if you ask her brother. I'm seeing you with your two half-sisters, laughing, talking, having a great time. I know you'll meet them soon. But your mom feels like she's tarnished."

"That's so right," Belle confirmed. "In fact maybe that's why I feel so numb. She puts on this big act, this big front of holier-than-thou, but I know it's because of the way she was treated by her grandmother and mother when she became pregnant with me.

Apparently, they were just horrible. But, she chose to hang on to that. I'd like to have her in my life, but I'm glad I'm in California and she's in Colorado. It really feels like, for years, she's been draining stuff out of me. Is that possible?"

"Yes. It's not just metaphysical. It's scientific that we're made up of energies. And definitely people can drain our energies."

Belle went on, "I even feel that my fears about driving come from her. Fearful to be alone. All these fearful things that don't gel with who I am and who I've been all my life. It's almost like somehow psychically I've pulled that in."

"You are so intuitive and you so wanted her. You were resonating with her energy even though you never realized it. So you were picking up on her energies."

"Somehow, I just get the feeling that she'd be thrilled if I dried up and blew away. I think I'm a thorn in her side. I don't think she looks at it from a healing aspect, I think she feels people will be looking at her life again. She's pathetic, a real sad case. I feel that she's part of the reason why my whole being is sort of on hold. I'm still going through our meeting in my mind, and I'm still not ready to talk to very many people about it. For 48 years, this has been going on and I need to do some healing with it. I feel sorry for her. She's so emotionally wrapped up in something that happened almost half a century ago. The only person putting guilt and shame on her is her. I'm not blaming her."

"Your adoptive dad is here saying, 'Much is going to change in your life because of all of this. Continue your search. This has been the source of many of your problems. Now that you've met her and were disappointed, you'll get on with your life. Now you'll start to realize that we weren't that bad."

Belle laughed. "I thought about that several times while we were meeting. They really weren't that bad. It's just that it seemed like my mother picked on me constantly. I just could not please the woman."

"Well, I feel you're going to see a real positive change in your marriage. For you in general, but for your marriage in particular."

"So how is John doing?" she asked, referring to her husband.

"He loves you very much. He was very happy to be there and be part of this meeting with you."

"Oh, really?"

"His higher self says that he feels like he can't be everything you want him to be. You don't lean on him as much as he'd like you to, and he felt the real need in you during that meeting with your Mom. That was a very warm time for him, a very loving time."

"Yes, I kind of got that impression."

"His protective instincts really came to the surface."

Comments on Belle

In Belle's case, she's not only able to hear the spirit sound of her loved ones, but very often, she feels their touch physically or other sensations through me. I'm able to act as her channel from one side of the veil to the other. The sound Belle's father makes is always tremendously loud. His spirit commands our attention!

When you've been adopted, as Belle was, you know what adoptive parents you're going to end up with before you incarnate. Again, there are no accidents or coincidences. Your biological parents are just the vehicle to give you the genetics you need for this incarnation.

Forgive-and-release is in order with not only Belle's adoptive parents, but also with her biological parents. Besides the balloon technique, I often use another very effective method:

Write a letter expressing all your pent-up emotions. This is what I call "a hate letter." Once again, as with the balloon technique, put on some soothing music, take the phone off the hook, put yourself in an altered state of consciousness, and taking deep breaths, knowing that every time you exhale you're getting rid of all stress, anger and fears, and that every time you inhale, you're breathing in peace, joy, serenity, and unconditional love. Then relax your body one part at a time.

Next, let yourself float backwards in time. For instance, Belle could write a hate letter to her adoptive mom, whom she felt never bonded with her and whom she could never please no matter what she did. She needs to float herself back into childhood and call on her guardian angel and her guides to help her to release these pent-up emotions once and for all.

Then write everything the other person did or didn't do to you. Sometimes what they didn't do is worse than what they did do. Don't mail the letter—that would just cause more karma. Then, read the letter every day. It may take a month, or if it's deeply ingrained hurt, it may take several months or longer. But one day while reading it, you may say, "Yes! I said that strongly enough. Another day, you may think, "I didn't say that strongly enough." So, cross it out and rewrite it.

This brings all your emotions up and out of your body and into the universe. If you leave these emotions in, they have to get out of you somehow, often in the form of a physical illness. This is an extremely therapeutic exercise. Do it before the stuck energy manifests as an illness.

Then, one day as you read this letter, you'll feel a shift of consciousness and realize that you've finally been able to release this person. Then, write across the letter, "I forgive and release you!"

We don't have to condone, but we do need to forgive. Again, have your higher self forgive their higher self. That way, you're not dealing with the personalities or characters of those involved. Then crinkle up the paper and throw it out, or burn it—both are symbolic of releasing.

I've seen clients heal themselves of long term illnesses using either of these forgive-and-release techniques.

39. Kay

At our yearly toy party meeting in Boston, Kay sat by me during lunch. "What do you do besides toys?" she asked. That question opened up a whole new world for her since she had never been involved with anything metaphysical up to that point in her life.

"There's a man standing beside you," I told her and described him.

"That's my brother-in-law, Charles. He died two years ago."

"He's saying to me, 'I was in Boston one day, San Jose the next day and then Chicago. The price was right and it's the only way to travel.'"

"I'm concerned about my daughter's house selling. She'd been happily married for one year but then her husband was killed in a freak industrial accident. She's anxious to sell their house. Charles and I always used to talk about going into real estate together."

"Charles is telling me, 'Hilary's house will sell when the mums are in bloom.'"

Kay attended an automatic writing class I gave in Colorado. *Side note: one of the participants was trying to hold her pencil in her right hand since she is right-handed, but her left hand kept twitching. She finally transferred the pencil to her left hand and the writing started immediately. It turned out to be a sixth grade friend of hers who has crossed over, and the friend had been left-handed.*

Kay's father came through her writing, and he wrote his police badge number in the middle of the page. That was the most obvious way he could think of for her to know it was him.

Kay has many such stories to tell of different friends who have had readings from me, but her personal story began when she and her daughter, Hilary, flew from Chicago to San Jose to attend my "Beginning Your Intuitive Search" seminar.

In reading for her, I described a man who she identified as her dad. Every time he came through me that week, I found myself humming *Sweet Gypsy Rose*. That meant nothing to her at the time, but when her brother heard about it, he turned absolutely white and said that their dad was always humming that song.

On the same trip, Kay was sleeping in my daughter's bedroom and her uncle (who is on the other side) called her name out loud.

That got her attention.

Kay and Hilary met up with her son and his wife when they returned to Chicago and were discussing the week they'd spent with me in San Jose. They were telling them about how the spirits liked to communicate through electricity. At that moment, all the lights in the condo went out and the only sound to be heard was her son swallowing nervously. He asked with a shaky voice, "How often does this happen?"

"Up to now, never," Kay laughed. A minute or so later, the lights came back on.

Comments on Kay

Kay automatically assumed that Hilary's house would sell in the spring (because of the flowers), and was extremely disappointed when spring came and went and nothing happened. But, the day Hilary actually sold the house, Kay and her husband noticed a house on the corner with a front yard packed with mums in full bloom.

Late one afternoon, I answered the door to find a florist's delivery man with a gigantic mum plant. The card on the plant simply read, "Mums in bloom, house sold!"

40. Jan

Jan was quite skeptical when she first walked in. This was her first experience with anyone who talked to the spirit realm. We had never met before and I knew nothing about her, not even her last name, but I told her things that nobody but her could know, and she left the reading a firm believer.

In Jan's reading, the first spirit that came was her mom, and Jan was surprised to actually feel her presence in the room. "She's telling me, 'It's very important for you to know that I really did love you very much but I just couldn't seem to show you any affection.'"

Vanishing Veil

She went on to give Jan many messages that explained so many things that the two of them had disagreed on. Jan explained, "The loss of my mother is still hard for me to accept. I miss her very much. I can't put into words how much you've helped me release so many angry feelings I had inside that were tearing me apart. That put my mind at peace about my mother's love for me."

Afterwards, Jan told me, "My mother and I weren't close when I was growing up. She didn't show me any love or affection. I really was an unhappy child. When she was sixty-three, she was diagnosed with lung cancer and within a month, it had spread to her brain.

"I was divorced at the time so I moved in with her to take care of her. During the six months that I took care of her before she died, I really tried to work things out. I felt so guilty, feeling that maybe I hadn't tried hard enough when I was younger. Although I did everything for her as an adult and was always there for her, still I never felt she loved me. The last month was the hardest for me, she needed total care. I kept telling myself, 'She'll realize how much I love her and she'll tell me she loves me.' But she died without telling me. I was devastated. I kept thinking, 'Mom, why didn't you love me?' It haunted me like a plague."

After her reading, Jan attended my beginner's seminar. In the automatic writing segment, she was still skeptical until her hand just started moving on its own and wrote, "Mom loves you."

After the astral flight I took the class on, Jan reported, "When you told us someone we knew would be floating up next to us, I saw my Mom and she embraced me. I actually felt her physically and she told me that she really did love me."

"Ever since that seminar," Jan told me, "I've done a lot of automatic handwriting, and my mother is one of the main people who gives me messages. Mainly we talk about my family, especially my brothers and my sister, who is a street person, a drug addict and an alcoholic. I've contacted my father-in-law, who I was very close to and my grandmother. I communicate with them all the time. This opened up channels for me to talk with whoever I want on the other side. I like automatic handwriting best because it's all documented."

Comments on Jan

It's devastating to lose anyone, but when you develop your sixth sense which, trust me, we all have, you can become aware of their presence. Better yet, you can learn to contact them, and it helps tremendously to transcend the grief.

Even though it's extremely difficult when you feel that a parent doesn't love you, know that this is not a random universe. Nothing happens without a larger purpose or without your consent. So, try to see the bigger picture.

Above all, don't think that anything was done to you. It's all right to feel a little victim energy for a while in order to clear it from your energy fields, but letting "victim" become a part of your identity doesn't serve you. It holds you back from getting on with your life.

41. Katy

"The first spirit here for you is a big man with reddish colored hair and a beautiful smile. He's standing right behind you and he has his hands on your shoulders."

"That's my father," Katy said, looking around.

"Can you feel his hands?"

"Well, I feel really touched inside. Really moved. I don't physically feel it. But, I feel his presence."

"He's telling me to tell you that he loves you and that he is with you. He is one of your spirit guides. There's someone else here who's still living."

I described her and Katy said, "That's my grandma."

"Her higher self is telling you that she doesn't have much time left on earth, and you should enjoy her while you can."

Vanishing Veil

Later that day, Katy called me to say, "When I left your house, I was driving home and there was a song playing on the radio with the lyrics, *I will always be there*. I was so busy listening to that I got lost and ended up on a street called 'James Street.' That's my dad's first name. I thought that was really weird because I've never heard of a 'James Street' before. It really affected me because I felt that maybe he directed me there so that I would realize that you were right and he really was still around.

"Hearing that my dad still existed really helped me a lot. It can be such a darkness if you feel that someone you love no longer exists. It's really hard to deal with that. Just feeling him, his presence, his love, really helped me. And just feeling that I could call on him, and knowing that he hadn't abandoned me was wonderful. Since that reading I feel like I can tune into him."

"How old were you when your dad died?" I asked.

"I was seventeen. He died the night I graduated from high school. He had a sudden heart attack. I went into my parents' bedroom and he wasn't breathing. My mother was there. I don't even know why I went into their bedroom. It was like one in the morning and their light was on. And there he was, not breathing. I tried CPR, but when the paramedics came, they said he was dead.

"It just devastated me. I had a breakdown and couldn't control my emotions. I just felt really, really sick. I don't know how to explain it."

"Did you ever end up in a hospital because of it?"

"Not right away, although I really should have gone. My mother chose to ignore what was happening to me. I had been pretty out-going, the type of person who pretty much succeeded in everything I tried. I was real popular in school, and suddenly all I could do was stay in bed all day. It was as though I'd just been short-circuited. I wondered if maybe I picked up on some of what he was experiencing when he died and it was kind of a shock to my system. Could that be possible?"

"Oh, sure it is. You just tuned into his frequency."

"I felt light around myself for a couple of weeks after dad's death. I didn't know what that meant."

"You experienced the wonderful light of God and that just doesn't dissipate when you came back. What a beautiful experience."

A year or so after that reading, Katy called to say, "My grandmother was killed in a fire soon after my reading. She's made her presence known to me and my mother a few times since then. On the first anniversary of the fire, a picture of her that had been in one of bedrooms for a long time came flying off the wall in the middle of the night. That was at my Mom's house, and that same night, I had a dream about her in which she was talking to me. It's odd since I hadn't dreamed about her since the fire."

"Did she have a message? Can you remember what she said?"

"She said that she was living with Dan, her man at the end of this life. He died about six years ago. She said that he really fixed her place up real nice and that she wanted me to come and visit. I got kind of confused."

"Well, you know, Katy, you can go and visit. You can astrally fly there at night or while in meditation. Ask before you go to sleep to be able to recall the visit."

"I'm confused. Could she really have a house over there?"

"Oh yes, they really do have houses over there."

"They do?"

"I often hear the spirits saying things like, 'I live in a little cottage,' or, 'I have a big house on a hill.' In fact, they will often show me their dwelling place. Or, if they enjoyed gardening on earth, they may talk about their garden."

"Oh, really?"

"Yes, you can have whatever you want over there. The energy on the earth plane is a lot denser than on the other side of the veil. When we visualize and try to make something happen, it takes us longer and we tend to get impatient because we want everything to happen right away. Well, on the other side of the veil, all you have to do is to think of something and it manifests immediately.

You can literally change houses or change the view from your house just by visualization."

"I've seen some movies like that. So when low-life types die, do they get absorbed into the darkness? Do they ever come out?"

"Yes, they do go into the dark shadows, and yes, they can come out. But they're in such a low space for such a long time that they don't even remember that there's such a thing as the Light of God. So, they just put themselves there and many of them stay there for a long time."

Comments on Katy

There is no such thing as a coincidence. The song that played on the radio as Katy left my house after her reading was definitely meant for her to hear. And then, getting lost and finding herself on James Street, the name of her father—again, no accident. These are the ways your loved ones, guardian angels and spirit guides talk to you. She needed confirmation that she truly was making contact with her father after all those years.

When you ask for guidance while in meditation and you don't seem to receive your answer immediately, become aware that everything talks to you. It may be the lyrics of a song on a radio as in Katy's case, or maybe the title of the song itself. A book may fall off a shelf at the library that is exactly what you need to read at the moment. Or, you may be dusting a book and it falls open to a page, and when you start reading that page, it's the answer you were looking for. Or, as you're driving down the road, a billboard you pass may have a message for you. Once you ask for guidance, everything speaks to you.

42. Jennifer

Jennifer had been to me for at least three readings without bringing a tape recorder. The next time she came, she brought one and opened a brand new pack of tapes she had just bought. At that time, I wasn't yet taping my readings and welcomed Jennifer taping the reading.

When she got home, she listened to the tape and was amazed to hear dozens of voices laughing, talking and having fun. What she heard was completely different from the reading she'd had, so she called me. I asked her to bring the tape back so that we could listen to it together.

"To me, it sounds as if we were downstairs and there was a party going on upstairs. I can hear their voices very clearly but can't specifically make out what they're saying."

"Yes, that's how it sounds to me, although a couple different times, I can hear my mom say in a real high-pitched voice, 'I'm so proud of you.' There's no question about what she said. It was high, shrill and fast, but very distinct."

"I also saw your dad actually plugging in a tape recorder on the other side, because he wanted so badly to get that message across."

"My mother's statement was a new experience for me, since she'd always been very verbal about what was wrong with me, but not so regarding her feelings. So, this message was real significant.

"Your dad said that his brother was spending a lot of time on the other side at that time and would be staying there permanently soon." (Jennifer's uncle crossed over about three or four months later.)

I asked Jennifer if I could have a copy of the tape so that I could play it at my seminars so my students could actually hear the voices of the spirits. She took it several places to try to get it duplicated, and no studio could duplicate it. Although Jennifer played that tape countless times for close friends and her daughter, it would play back only on one tape player—the one she used in the reading!

The tape contained another useful piece of information for Jennifer. She told me, "At the time, my husband and I were having a power struggle between our relationship and our business. Other family members worked in the business, but my husband didn't want to be involved so we plunged ahead without him. The higher self of one my brothers appeared on the tape to say, "Your husband really does love you and things will work out."

"Did it all work out for you?" I asked.

"Yes. No one in the family is still involved with the business, but we realized that relationships are more important than any business, and we were able to keep our relationship intact during and after the transition. But, again, he wasn't one to verbalize feelings, so it was nice to get that reassurance."

That tape doesn't play anymore and the tape recorder no longer works. Jennifer played that tape over and over, until she felt there was no more to be gotten from it. Then it was gone. But for several months, she could go back and play it whenever she wanted.

Comments on Jennifer

This is a clear-cut case where the sound of the spirits and her mother's message were meant for her ears only, and a few hand-picked friends, and were not to be used at my seminars.

Again, this was performed over a piece of electrical equipment, which, for some reason, is easy for the spirits to come through. It was truly amazing to hear since Jennifer and I were the only two in my house at the time of her reading and the house was otherwise silent.

43. Kari

When she arrived at my regular monthly meeting, Kari reported that she was experiencing waves of extreme anxiety, even fear. As it happened, I was conducting a group clearing that night. The notion that spirits could easily "jump into" living people was new to her, for now ...

I put the group into a deep, relaxed meditative state and asked any spirits within group members to remember their names. Kari clearly heard the name "Betty." She picks up the story in her own words.

"I wondered who among the group might be acquainted with someone named Betty. Suddenly, I became aware that I couldn't feel my hands and my back felt very hot so I missed what Marge was saying.

"When I heard her talking about seeing the God light, I saw a light so bright that I wanted to squint my eyes. I realized that was ridiculous because my eyes were already shut and I knew Marge had darkened the room.

"Next, Marge invited the spirits to stick their hands toward the light and I visualized the hand of an elderly woman reaching toward the light, only as I looked, it changed to a younger woman's hand. This impressed me because I often try too hard to visualize during meditations.

"I also saw two other entities but can't really describe them. They held a beautiful, gilded full-length mirror just in front of me. (Marge had asked someone in the spirit world to hold a mirror for the spirits inhabiting us.) Then I saw, standing by the mirror, a woman, maybe in her forties, with her black hair swept back. She was wearing a lovely royal-blue and black two-piece suit.

"When Marge brought us out of our relaxed state, I shared part of what I had seen but said I didn't really understand all that I'd seen and experienced. Marge, however, said that she saw that Betty had been a spirit inside me. That made sense when I remembered odd times when bizarre thoughts would cross my mind such as, 'What would it be like if ....' They were always unpleasant, negative thoughts about material temptations or doing something dishonest. I feel strongly that the Betty spirit was the source.

"In 1985, I was in the hospital for an appendectomy, and in 1990, I visited a funeral home to see my grandmother. A spirit could have attached itself to me on either occasion."

Comments on Kari

Clients often experience "spirit resistance" to a clearing as Kari did when she felt the extreme anxiety. Spirits are obviously threatened by an upcoming clearing. So the fear that Kari experienced was the fear from the intruding entity (Betty) who had merged with her.

44. Susan

Susan first came to see me in Chicago for a reading, regression and seminar in March 1987. She was incredibly nervous meeting me. Even though a friend had told her a lot about me, she was still skeptical and nervous. We met the night before the seminar began and both of us had an instant feeling of camaraderie. I later confided in her that I felt she had been my daughter in a past life, and knew we were supposed to meet up again in this life. No wonder there was a strong pull between us!

At one point that first evening, about seven of us were sitting around the kitchen table and I started describing an older lady, and Susan said, "That's my grandmother."

After a dialogue with her grandmother, Susan became a believer. She said, "There's only one way you could have done this, and that's if you'd actually seen her because you described her exactly as I remembered her. She told you little things like that I'd never seen her wear pants, and they were all correct. She died when I was in the second grade, and I felt her loss very profoundly. But I was not allowed to go to her funeral. I could only watch it from my classroom window. I always had deep regrets about all that, so getting in contact with her has made a lot of things better for me."

At the end of the seminar that Susan attended, she said, "The most significant thing I got out of it was learning and enjoying that I could make contact with the higher selves of people who are still here, even more so than on the other side. This helps when you have feelings for people but can't figure out why, or there are things that you'd like to say to people but can't muster up the courage. Now I enjoy being able to communicate with them telepathically on this higher level. In a lot of my readings when you tapped into the higher selves of my friends, your insight made sense of a lot of things I didn't fully understand in my various relationships."

During the seminar, I also did a reading for Susan's mother and psychically saw her leaving the house and slamming the door. I told her, "I'm seeing that your relationship with your husband will be very different from now on. I'm sensing lots of anger."

She was really upset about the reading, but Susan later told me, "Marge, you pegged her exactly right. How can she pretend she doesn't have all that anger?"

Months later, Susan told me, "My mother had a brain aneurysm and she literally, on a mental level, slammed that door and checked out, so to speak, on her husband, and the rest of her family for that matter. When she first got sick, I used the mental telepathy technique you'd taught us to contact her higher self and help me to make sense of what was going on because, at that point, she was no longer able to communicate with us."

Another time, I gave a reading for Susan's sister-in-law, Donna, while her three-month-old baby was asleep on the couch in the same room. During Donna's reading, I told her, "There's a protective spirit here for little Jacqueline, and right now, this spirit is hovering directly over her."

At exactly that moment, the baby, who had been peacefully sound asleep, looked up over her head and smiled, and then looked at me and Donna, smiled and promptly went back to sleep again as if to say, "Yes, it's true!"

When Donna was about seven months pregnant with her twins, she and her husband, Billy, were having some weird things happening in their home, where they felt the presence of spirits. Even though Billy was totally skeptical, even he admitted that something strange was occurring. The presence felt very negative and was really starting to scare them. One night, thirteen-month-old Jacqueline was in her room crying as if really scared. Billy and Donna were also scared, so they called their dog in for courage and the three of them went into the baby's room. The dog immediately ran back out again and wouldn't return.

Donna knew there was a spirit in the room, and shouted, "I don't know who you are or what you're doing but you're scaring us. Get out of here and just leave us alone!"

With that, the baby stopped crying so they went back into their bedroom. A few minutes later, the baby was just laughing and giggling, as if someone was playing with her. They got up and checked on her and she was smiling and happy.

Donna went into the hospital the next day and had twins, two months prematurely! She was sure that it was the twins who were making baby Jacqueline laugh the night before. I was later able to confirm that the spirits of the twins had come early to visit Jacqueline.

About two years later, Susan attended another of my seminars in which I took the group through a regression into a past life. She told me afterwards, "When you were discussing regressions into this life, you told us about a woman you regressed who'd been sexually abused by her stepfather until she was eleven years old, and yet she'd suppressed it. But, when you regressed her, she relived it. As you were speaking, I had an overwhelming feeling that it had happened to me, too, but I didn't have any solid memories. My only memory had to do with me saying or thinking, 'No, I don't want this to happen again!' I'd have this thought whenever I'd see one of my uncles. He is about seven years older than me. So, in the seminar, I thought, 'Oh my God, now what do I do? I need to deal with this.' "

When the group returned from dinner late that night, I told Susan, "You need to be regressed back into childhood to know for sure if you were indeed molested, so you can start working on releasing it. I was flying home early the next morning, so about 2:30 in the morning, I regressed her.

Here's Susan, in her own words: "I saw so many vivid incidents that I had to face that it really happened. It was still incredibly difficult to face it though. I was in the first grade and my grandmother was very, very, sick. In fact, she was dying at her home. My uncle, my Dad's younger brother, was proving extremely hard for her to control, so she had him move in with us. My folks put an extra bed in my bedroom for him. During the regression, I saw that he had forced me into oral sex and intercourse."

During the regression, his mother (my grandmother, who is dead) showed up and told me that what Susan was seeing was true, and that she was very sad about the whole thing and it should never have happened.

During another reading for Susan, she brought a lot of photographs of handicapped children who she worked with. One spirit in particular showed up—a little autistic boy who seemed to be very distressed. Susan told me, "His early childhood was just hell. He could never figure out what was going on. He was always so confused. This was very stressful for him. He's a beautiful little boy. He and I have this incredible emotional link. We always have."

When I held his photo and picked up his vibrations, he screamed in my head, "I want to get out of my body. I made a mistake and wish I hadn't done this to myself. This is much harder than I thought it would be."

With a photo of another autistic child, I heard from his higher self, "I've done this many times with one handicap or another because it's good for all the people around me, besides growing spiritually in leaps and bounds myself."

In yet another reading, Susan showed me a picture of a good friend of hers who was planning her wedding. Everything I picked up from her energy was negative. I told Susan, "The relationship she's in is really terrible, nothing is going right, and she's in a really bad situation. But, I feel she will get herself out of it."

Susan protested, "No way. You're wrong. She's in the middle of all these wonderful wedding plans."

The friend ended up canceling the wedding twice, but then

going ahead with it. They were divorced in less than a year.

Susan later told me, "I've done some great releasing of people from my emotional field with things that I learned at your first two seminars. One day, I made a long list of people in my life and what about each of them bothered me. I did this in a beautiful, quiet park, which was a perfect place to do it. Then I went into a meditative state and one by one talked to them mentally. I explained all the deep-seated feelings and hurts I had with them but had been unable to say to their faces. It was a wonderful release. You have really put me in touch with this whole release process, which as you say, is so important for getting on with your life.

"Through your seminars, I realized that there are all these plans out there that I on some level did have some stake in making, even though, when things aren't going as well as I'd like, it's hard to accept that! Opening up to this whole metaphysical world put me on my spiritual path. I even found the strength to move by myself from Illinois to Colorado, something that wouldn't have happened before I became involved with you. More likely, I would have, to quote you, 'stayed stuck in my story.'

"Opening up to metaphysics has also helped me to form bonds with my group of friends that I don't think we ever would have been able to form—intimacy on the spiritual level that we never had before.

"One final story: A friend and I had just watched the movie *Ghost*. As we pulled out of our parking spot, we felt a bump as if we'd run over someone's feet. We looked at each other and didn't say a word."

The next time Susan had a phone reading with me, a friend of hers who had recently been killed in a motorcycle accident showed up and sat on the edge of my desk talking to me and laughing about the prank he'd pulled on Susan and her friend. "I just wanted to see if I could contact them."

"Well he did!"

Comments on Susan

Picking up on the energy of the photo is called psychometry. Become aware that when you're holding a photo of someone, that you're picking up on their vibrations. Tune into any feelings or thoughts that you're having.

45. Lucy

The first person I described for Lucy was her grandmother who'd just died the month before.

"She's sitting on the couch beside you," I told her. "She's leaning on you and wrapping her arms around you."

"I know it isn't the power of suggestion," Lucy said. "I definitely feel the pressure of her body leaning on me and her warmth."

"She was more of a mother to you than your own mother, wasn't she?" I asked.

"That's definitely true!" Lucy confirmed.

"I'm seeing that you wanted to come to her as one of her children, but she couldn't have any more, so, your next best choice was to wait and come to one of her children. I am seeing your abusive childhood—verbal, physical, and sexual—at the hands of both your mother and father, and that the only light in your tunnel was your grandma. She has decided to become one of your guides, and eventually, you will become very aware of her presence."

Lucy later told me that this has since happened.

The second to appear was the higher self of someone alive and well in Lucy's life. When I described him, she confirmed that it was her husband.

"I'm seeing that he is physically, mentally, and verbally abusive to you," I told her.

"Now, I'm seeing another man," I said, and I described him.

"He's a married man who I've been seeing for over eleven years," she confessed.

"I can see that," I said. "And that he'll never leave his wife,

185

mostly because of finances. You appear to be totally in love with him, and he loves you in his own way, but not as deeply or sincerely as yours. He is very clever and knows just what to say to keep you under his control."

Later, Lucy told me ruefully, "Looking back, I should have realized that myself."

"Why don't we do a regression and go back to see why you're attracting this type of situation into your life. It seems like you want a man on one level, yet subconsciously you attract someone you can't have."

After the regression, Lucy told me, "I realize now that it has to do with the relationship between me and my father. He molested me many times as a child, and because of this, I have mixed feelings about men and how they love me."

After taking a series of classes, Lucy was pleased to tell me, "I've been able to forgive my father for what he did and I've also found a greater respect for myself. It's helped me realize that I am a good person and I don't deserve someone using me. I now realize I do have control over what's happening in my life. Also, I now know how to get in touch with my spiritual guides, who have helped me through many rough times and have given me good advice.

"I've been able to get a lot of messages from automatic handwriting. This is a great way to communicate with the other side, as it keeps records of what I'm told. I don't always get perfectly accurate answers, but it's a way of communicating with my loved ones on the other side. That in itself has been very comforting to me.

"Breaking up with my married friend has been very difficult. Our relationship didn't happen overnight and I couldn't just break it off overnight. But, I feel I'm on the right track. Before, I kept myself all for him, and in fact, I finally left my husband for him. I've learned that if you really work on bringing in good things to your life and getting rid of someone or something that's causing you grief, your life definitely improves. I'm now open for a new relationship."

Comments on Lucy

Lucy has since broken off her relationship with her married friend and found her true soul-mate once she'd forgiven and released her dad. Again, we don't have to condone, but we do need to have our higher self, or God within, forgive the other's higher self or God within. Otherwise we keep doing as Lucy did. Her conscious mind kept telling her she wanted a man, while her subconscious mind kept saying, "You don't want a man, look at what one did to you when you were a child." So her subconscious mind kept drawing in men who were unavailable to her.

People like Lucy's father and husband, who create pain in others, who are aggressive, bully people and make life miserable for those around them are usually the most in need of love.

When you can think of your childhood and your parents and know that they did the best they could, considering their childhood and their situation, you are then free of your past. As you change your negative memories into positive understanding, you can go even faster into your new future. Your parents may have developed your strength, or your inner will, by creating obstacles for you.

We choose our parents, race, country and our gender on our evolutionary pathway. All the relationships and all the people in your world are there because you attracted or chose them. They are helping you to fulfill something you need to learn, even those who seem to "do it to you." Once you understand that everyone in your world is only acting out the script that you handed them, you'll understand that you can change the script. We co-create our reality.

Sometimes the lesson in a relationship is how to hang in there and try to work things out. Other times, the lesson to be learned is how to exit a situation that doesn't serve you.

The *Course in Miracles* tells us, "Forgiveness is selective remembering. It's a conscious decision to focus on love and let the rest go."

We can't change someone else, but we can change ourselves. So, when someone is projecting to you, do not resist it but look at it as something you need to learn. However, that is often difficult because it means taking responsibility for everything that happens to you, including when people "do it to you." Believing that everything is happening for your higher good renders negative energy harmless.

When someone is showing you something you don't like, it's a message for you. Don't get "stuck in your own story" but look at the message behind a problem. If you respond to the garbage going on, you keep it there.

Sometimes you need to let go of a relationship, a job or a way of life. Learn to open to the new and release the old when it no longer serves you. Everything comes into your life to teach you something. When a person, situation or job has taught you all it can, your higher self will replace it with something that will offer you new opportunities to grow and evolve.

We attract situations into our lives to learn from them. One way out and up is by responding with love. As you do so, every situation will change in its nature and character. Practice everywhere you go, sending love to the earth, sending love to those you meet, including complete strangers as well as those who cause you pain.

Become aware when someone's presence leaves you drained. Don't put yourself around anyone who wants to drain or use your energy. Loving someone does not mean making his or her feelings more important than your own. Being committed to your higher purpose and loving to yourself is the first priority. Know that you do not owe anyone your time or energy. They are the greatest gift you have been given, and how you use them will determine how much you will evolve in this lifetime.

Be very selective about people whose company you keep. Find people who are coming from a higher level of awareness.

46. Jasmine

The following is what is called a near death experience, or NDE. Jasmine was in California visiting a daughter and two sisters, and she made an appointment to have a regression to see if she could get more detail on her beautiful experience.

In the fall of 1989, when Jasmine was forty-two years old, she was diagnosed with a rare form of blood cancer. She also has breast cancer. It all began when she went in for a general physical because she had a sensation that something was going on in her body. Once in the hospital, she clinically "died" and spent two weeks unconscious in intensive care, during which time, she had the following experience.

"I remember saying to myself, 'I am ready to go now,' and then I left my body. With no emotion or concern, I hovered over myself and the doctors. I was just an observer. Then I flew down the corridors of the hospital and out of the hospital. I went to what I can only describe as a house with many rooms and I was supposed to observe all of these individuals doing different things in different rooms. This went rather slowly, still no emotion or concern.

"Then I flew across the country very low to the ground to Big Sur in California—my most favorite place. From there, I went feet first at lightning speed through a tunnel of liquid gold and liquid blue colors towards a bright white light. As I came into the light, it changed from white to a golden glow. I sensed nothing but love and light.

"Suddenly, I was on a large hilltop covered with green meadow and flowers, where I was greeted by my parents, my brother and my grandparents. They all appeared exactly as I remembered them last, before illness, and they were dressed normally. Behind them were millions of individuals wearing gowns of some kind, but no real faces or human characteristics, just beings. I had a feeling they were past generations of mine. Again, love and warmth prevailed and I had no concerns.

"Suddenly a bridge appeared in front of me and my mother

came across. She told me telepathically, 'It is not yet your time. You have some things to take care of—Audrey (my youngest girl) and Dan (my husband)—before you can return.'

"I wanted to stay but wasn't upset to go back. Then I heard the sound of beautiful voices or music coming from the beings behind my parents. As the sound got louder and louder, it became more and more beautiful. I felt as if I was told so many things. I saw beams of light coming up to these individuals from space or time and I was told that these were prayers for me.

"Then suddenly I was back and excitedly blurted out to my surgeon every little detail of my trip. As soon as the words came out I realized where I had been and what happened to me to put me there, and we both cried. The doctors were amazed I pulled through, but I knew it was meant to be. Whenever I feel down, I just go back to that wonderful day."

When Jasmine came to California to visit relatives, her sister made an appointment for her with me so that I could take her back through her near-death experience to see if she could remember any more details. However, she was skeptical because she never thought she could be hypnotized.

In the regression, she experienced the exact same events, but then there was a surprise for her. I asked her, "Is there someone there with you?"

"I don't know," she replied.

"At the count of three, turn around and tell me what you see," I asked.

"It's an angel," she gasped. "It's got a hand on my shoulder, and it's the most beautiful being I had ever seen."

At that moment, she started trembling all over and I thought she was going to have a seizure so I brought her out of trance right away. Once she was out, she said, "I was told that all people will meet again in another dimension. Upon death, what you will experience depends whatever faith or belief you have. The key to all this is love. Once someone has this love in their heart, they will be able to step into this dimension. Also there are no coincidences—everyone just needs to be more aware and find the hidden answers. I have many tasks to take care of, one of which is helping others by sharing my knowledge."

She later added, "Since my NDE, I have a totally new outlook on life and my priorities. I awake every morning and am happy and thankful for all I see, say and do. I meditate diligently and this has helped me through so many stressful situations and procedures.

"Currently I am vice-president of a local chapter of the American Cancer Society and have started a support group for cancer survivors and their families, helping people to be informed and to take charge of their lives. I tell them to keep a smile on their face, take one day at a time, have a positive attitude and learn the healing power of the higher self.

"Cancer has given me a sudden sense of my mortality, that I'm not going to live forever, that my life has very suddenly become quite finite. Things that once seemed 'unimportant' now seem very important. I have a new appreciation for the wonderment of life.

"I am spreading the word that there is a 'light at the end of the tunnel.' That phrase is often over-used nowadays, but I can vouch for the fact that the 'light' truly awaits us when we return 'home.' "

47. Karla

Karla has had two regressions with me and both have cured serious physical ailments for her. In the first, during a hypnotherapy seminar I gave, I asked the group to pair up and pick an issue from their lives that they wanted to resolve. Since there was an odd number, I paired with Karla. She wanted to know why she was always struggling with her weight. She started putting it on after high school and has never managed to get below 30 pounds above her ideal weight. Nothing worked, so she wanted to discover what blocks she had around the weight issue.

Vanishing Veil

Here's what happened in her own words:

"I am a beautiful, little girl during the cowboy era. I live in a small, western town where everybody knows each other. I am about seven years old and am being molested by an old man who lives in the town. I am looking up at his ugly face—long gray hair pulled back in a ponytail, several front teeth missing, with the rest crooked and yellow. His face is deeply wrinkled and he always looks dirty. I am so frightened that I don't want to remember what he is doing to me. It is too awful to recall."

As Karla spoke, she was shaking lying on my couch. I asked her if she wanted to go back and really look at it. "No way," she said.

Finally, I convinced her that she could watch it as though it were a movie and not have to relive all the details. However, since she didn't want to see it, she stopped seeing the pictures and just received the information intuitively. Apparently, she knew that he molested and raped her for many years as she was growing up. He made terrible threats about what he would do to her and her family if she ever told anyone about what he was doing.

"Why did he single you out over all the girls in the town," I asked.

"Because I was so pretty," she replied. Beyond that, she didn't get any details because she chose not to.

We worked for a long time on releasing the old man's energies. I asked Karla's higher self (while still in a deep meditation) to explain how this life related to her current life. Her higher self said, "Because the old man chose her for her attractiveness, she carried over a fear of looking too pretty. So, as a protection against unwanted sexual advances, she put on a lot of weight."

That's a common story, I thought, but then Karla's higher self had a surprise for her about the timing of her weight gain. It told her, "You have completely suppressed the memory of how, during your sophomore year, you were molested on two separate occasions by older teenage boys. These unwanted encounters triggered the past life memories on a subconscious level which led to the weight gain. It had nothing to do with diet."

We worked on releasing the thought pattern that being attractive only invites trouble, and this allowed Karla to realize that she was no longer a helpless, frightened, little girl. She no longer needed to hide her true self under this disguise.

During the nine months after the regression, Karla slowly and steadily dropped ten pounds without changing anything in her diet. Then, unknown to one another, two friends encouraged her to read the same book on diet and health. Such "coincidences" are invariably significant, so she followed their suggestion. The book opened up a whole new world for her, and she turned vegetarian. Within three months and further health habit changes, she permanently dropped another 20 pounds.

Karla's second experience actually started two years ago when, one day, her neck just started hurting for no apparent reason. It got so bad that she couldn't turn her head to look over her shoulder or nod up and down, and sleep had become almost impossible. She tried every chiropractor in the phone book to no avail. Finally, a new chiropractor and spiritual healer told her, "This neck problem is related to past lives. The only permanent treatment will need hypnotherapy."

That brought Karla back to me. We found five different lives that involved issues with her neck and throat. In the first, her throat closed so tightly that she couldn't swallow. As she relived each life and released its energies, the lump would get smaller until the fifth life, when it disappeared completely. Here's what she experienced:

"I am living deep in the jungles of South America a long time ago. I am captured one day and forced into slavery. I am led around with a thick, scratchy rope tied around my neck. Now I am in another life, and am hung for being a villain. Now I am back with the ugly old man who molests me. As he rapes me, he holds me down and keeps me from screaming by pressing both of his thumbs into my neck. He wraps his hands around my throat and squeezes tight."

Vanishing Veil

By the time we finished the regression, Karla was amazed that she'd had five past lives all related to her neck and was anxious to see what the results would be. Over the next week, her neck started to feel progressively better. But, at a certain point, it leveled out and didn't heal completely. Feeling frustrated, she was talking about it with her massage therapist, also a student of mine.

Suddenly, as the therapist was massaging her head, chills swept through her and she had to step back from the table. "You're not done reliving all of your past lives on this issue. It just felt like your head was going to come off in my hands!"

The surprised Karla returned for another regression. She experienced more lifetimes:

"I am a dishonest politician. I go around the country giving speeches that totally deceive the public. Eventually, my lies catch up with me and I become the object of public scorn and ridicule. I end up feeling great shame for the way I have abused my power, and I manifest a tumor in my throat that grows so big that it eventually chokes out my life.

"I am now married to a king who has me beheaded because I am unable to bear children for him. My massage therapist in this life is my lady-in-waiting in that life and she witnesses my death. No wonder she felt as though my head was going to come off in her hands!"

Karla was amazed at how all of these different lives relate to aspects of her current life. For instance, she and her husband have had trouble conceiving children even though there is nothing medically wrong with either of them. Also, the lifetime in which the king had her killed embedded the belief in her subconscious that a woman's worth is related to her fertility.

The most profound understanding she received, however, came from connecting with her higher self and being able to look at all of her lives from a higher perspective. In some lifetimes, she had been the "bad guy" and in others, she had chosen to play the "victim."

But truly, there are no bad guys and no victims. We all chose the roles we want to play out in life because we need to learn different things and grow from them. Nobody does anything *to* us unless we choose on a higher level to have that experience for the purpose of spiritual advancement.

As Karla told me, "It really gave me a new way of looking at all the different players in my current life and appreciating them for all they have taught me—both the good and the bad. It makes it much easier to forgive others when you view things from this perspective. I even ended up thankful for my sore neck because it told me that I had to release, once and for all, a serious repeating pattern in all my lives. If I hadn't broken the pattern, it would have kept manifesting over and over again."

As a footnote, Karla's neck continued to heal slowly over the next few months after her final regression and has been completely normal for over a year.

48. Brianna

The month before Brianna's 30th birthday, she flew to Sedona to attend one of my seminars. The topic was healing, and she had come to work on her diabetes condition. However, she left the seminar with a whole lot more to think about!

"I was born chubby and never lost my so-called 'baby fat.' My life was a vicious circle—a messed up metabolism due to lack of exercise, lack of exercise due to asthma, asthma due to being overweight; need to exercise to lose weight to get rid of asthma. And somewhere along the line, I became a food addict!

"I ate when I was bored, angry, stressed, or depressed. I ate to celebrate. I couldn't stop, even when I wasn't hungry. Diet and exercise were no use. The problem was the inexplicable emptiness I felt inside, but not an emptiness due to hunger. It wasn't until a regression during the Sedona seminar that I discovered the invisible forces that were holding me prisoner.

"I grew up in a psychic household of past lives, reincarnation, and other concepts today labeled 'New Age,' so the ideas such as forgive-and-release, and letting go of past karma were not new to me. In fact, a psychic had already told my Mom that I was overweight in this life because I'd starved to death in a past life and was determined not to let that happen again. That insight, plus awareness of several past lives where my body was used sexually, explained why I used excess weight as a shield. I wasn't about to be used for my body again.

"So why, then, couldn't I lose the weight? I'd had this knowledge since my teenage years, so as an adult, why couldn't I simply rely on my intellect and good judgment to 'protect' me from unwanted or harmful sexual encounters? I knew it was because I still had an underlying fear that I hadn't yet been able to shake off. So I gave up on dieting and got used to living with my body, even though I longed for one that wasn't burdened with all the excess weight. Occasionally, I'd get angry at how my past lives still haunted me but, other than affirmations, I never did anything to forgive and release the past."

The final exercise of the healing seminar was a regression to lead attendees back to a childhood issue that gave rise to a current illness or condition. After relaxing the group and opening them to their higher selves, I took them back to the first time they encountered a situation that related to the current condition. Rather than focus on the diabetes, Brianna chose to focus on her excess weight, since she knew the weight was the root cause of the diabetes. This is what she found:

"I am a fourteen-year-old girl in Nazi Germany. The soldiers have just rounded me up with my family. The rest of my family is sent to a concentration camp, but the soldiers decide that since I am so delectably young and pretty, they will use me for their sexual pleasure. I feel tremendous guilt at being kept alive, while the rest of my family go off to meet certain death. And all because I am pretty. However, when the soldiers are through with me as their sex slave, I am sent to the concentration camp anyway, where I die of starvation."

Brianna later told me, "Another psychic told me about this lifetime when I was 21. It was one of those experiences when I knew what she was going to say before she said it. She told me, 'That lifetime was the source of the empty feeling that continually gnaws at your insides. Even though you chose loving parents in this lifetime, no amount of love can fill that empty feeling inside. That's why you sometimes get depressed and can't figure out why. It also explains why no amount of food or love can fill the void you feel. It's a void left from the despair, guilt, and shame of that lifetime in Nazi Germany.'

"For eight years, I've known of this past life and its impact on my current life. I thought that just knowing about it would let me get over it. Surely, my logical self should simply be able to take over and get me past this obstacle. Yet, here I am, in your seminar at the age of 29, grossly overweight and racked by the emotions of that other lifetime. Until this regression, I'd never allowed myself to relive it or go into it emotionally.

"Oh, I also uncovered another insight. The soldiers didn't pick me because of my looks. They picked me because they saw my spirit shining through. No matter what I looked like, they would have picked me. It was my light they craved, not my body. And when they discovered they couldn't capture my soul, they sent me away."

In the same regression, Brianna was taken back to age 14 in this lifetime. She was overweight but had been steadily losing the pounds, and was beginning to look good. Her sexual urges were becoming extremely strong, and she sensed that her beauty could easily get her into trouble if she continued to lose weight. Here's what she re-experienced:

"I am fourteen and my older sister is seventeen. Our parents return from visiting friends, where they'd discussed their friends' pregnant teenage daughter. Our parents tell us that if we ever get pregnant, they'll kick us out of the house in a heartbeat! My parents' words ring in my ears and, as a fourteen-year-old, I believe them and am terrified. Sexual energy is exploding within me, and I am being threatened with homelessness if I accidentally get pregnant!

"I panic and start to put weight back on. If I can't trust myself to refrain from having sex, then I will create a barrier so that no one will want to have sex with me. Obesity is an easy natural defense."

Comments on Brianna

Little did Brianna know at that time that the 14-year-old girl who was frightened of being attractive sexually in this lifetime had also brought forward the energy of a 14-year-old who had already been used sexually in another lifetime. No wonder the impact of her parents' declarations was so devastating.

Excessive weight often stems from a subconscious attempt to protect ourselves or feel safe from unwanted advanced from the opposite sex. However, Brianna left that seminar feeling like a weight had been lifted from her. Only time will tell if the forgive-and-release has totally freed her to finally lose all her excess weight and keep it off. But she certainly has a better chance now.

The process of leaving behind old habits begins with your thoughts. Albert Einstein once said, "Imagination is more important than knowledge." So, imagine yourself letting go of the obstacles you have chosen to experience in this lifetime. Know that you need no longer rely on those destructive patterns. Visualize the problem as a situation of the past. Look back at it and know that you no longer live that way. Realize the power of your thoughts. Know that whatever you can conceive in your mind you can bring into the physical world, including a slender body. The saying, "As you think, so shall you be," is accurate. So think thin!

We need to change our negative memories from this life and past lives into positive understanding. As we do, we release the pain. Focus your mind on what you can learn from each experience in your life.

Forgive yourself for past transgressions, both in this life and past lives, thus releasing many of the obstacles in your life.

Epilogue

With the energy shifts taking place in the universe now, and the dramatic increase in the population's awareness, none of us can do forgive-and-release processes enough. Notice how things from the past that have been buried for years within your subconscious mind are coming to the surface. They must be dealt with as they come up, by simply saying, "Thanks, universe for reminding me of that incident. I now release it and forgive the perpetrator. I also forgive myself for wanting or needing that situation or relationship in my life."

As hard as it is to imagine, remember that we draw these circumstances into our life so that we can grow from them. The one you need to forgive the most is yourself, but it's so much easier to blame others for our circumstances.

Your own previous thoughts—no one else's—created the reality you are now living. Listen to your mind chatter; it will explain the circumstances of your life. The first time I heard the term, "mind chatter," I listened in to mine. Now, I've always thought of myself as an extremely positive person, but I was appalled. I asked, "Who's that negative person in my head?" I then decided to dissipate that negativity. I told myself that, for the next three days, every time I heard negative mind chatter, I would repeat the word "love" until it dispelled. (Words have energies and the word "love" has a higher frequency than most, so saying "love" raised the frequency of my mind chatter). For three days, I walked around saying, "love, love, love, love."

This simple exercise made me more aware of my mind chatter. I'm human, so I still have negative or judgmental thoughts, but when I detect them, I now mentally say to the universe, "Neutralize that thought."

Know that thoughts are energy that creates our reality. Change your mind chatter and you'll change your life. Those of us who love each other the most can hurt each other the most through our thoughts. If we live with someone who is a slob, and we dwell on it, we're making that person more of a slob. What we think about, we make larger.

The universal law of attraction is that "Like attracts like." Think of how terrible your future will be if you're a negative thinker. You will draw into your life the very things that you think about the most. You always attract the qualities you possess, and what you think is what you become. If you express hatred, you will draw it to you. If you want peace and harmony in your life, you must become peaceful and harmonious.

If you focus on bringing out the good in other people, seeing their beauty and speaking to them of what you love about them, you will find the areas which were giving you problems beginning to resolve themselves, even though you haven't worked directly on finding solutions. The more you focus on problems between you and others, or on what is wrong with other people, the more you will find your relationships with them going downhill. When you pay attention to the positive, the good, in another person, you're helping them to create a good, positive life.

It's time to clear up our lives. If you're encountering some negativity in your life, go into an altered state of consciousness and ask to be shown the "bigger picture." Realize that you, on some level, brought this person or circumstance in your life. Find out what the lesson is that you wanted to learn from this person or situation, learn it and move on.

And finally, don't get stuck in your own story. Get rid of your fears of transition, of change. Know that we came to earth to grow spiritually. We grow through the lessons we draw to us, and often these are in the form of relationships. You are not truly growing if you allow yourself to become a victim or a martyr. Forgive and release whatever and whoever is holding you back so you can move forward. Don't let your feet get stuck in cement. Most important of all, forgive yourself.

About the Author

Photo by: Anne Knudsen

Since the late 1960's, Marge Cuddeback has given readings, regressions, clearings and seminars in California and across the nation. Her specialty has always been her psychic ability to see and communicate with spirits on the other side of the veil. She is also a certified hypnotherapist.

In addition to her BA in Education, she has degrees in Mari El and is a Reiki Master (both forms of holistic healing) and has been trained by two medical doctors who have quit their traditional practices and now heal with energies. Marge was in the toy party plan business for over 24 years and held positions in three different companies as District Manager, Vice President and President.

She has produced eight meditation tapes, has been on television, and is a frequent guest speaker on the radio in San Francisco, Santa Cruz, Santa Rosa, and Monterey.

She assists clients in their personal and spiritual growth. She is available to conduct seminars, readings, regressions and/or clearings.

She wishes to make everyone aware of their own power within, and looks forward to improving people's lives through her book.

Marge Cuddeback
6981 Elwood Rd.
San Jose, CA 95120
(408) 997-1869
margec@earthlink.net
www.margecuddeback.com

Meditation Tapes

MEDITATION AT THE BEACH - With the soothing sound of the ocean and seagulls in the background, you're led down the beach to meet up with your spiritual guide, guardian angel and/or a friend or relative who's crossed over to the other side, to either visit or receive your guidance.

RELATIONSHIPS - Marge gets you into an altered state of consciousness and then helps you to put out into the universe what you'd like in your long term relationship. Visualize what you want and make it happen!!

FORGIVE AND RELEASE - This forgive and release process helps you to put your past relationships behind you so they won't hold you back any longer. Until we go to the source, and forgive and release old relationships, we keep magnetizing similar types of relationships and circumstances into our life.

THUNDERSTORM MEDITATION - To the sound of thunder and rain, you're guided to a chalet on a mountain top to receive your guidance or simply enjoy the serenity as you sit in front of a fire watching the storm.

ASTRAL FLIGHT - This tape will give you the methods to more easily obtain out of body experiences. You will go to your place of choice.

MEDITATION TAPES

GETTING IN TOUCH WITH YOUR HIGHER SELF & CREATING YOUR OWN SANCTUARY - both sides are different on this tape. On both sides you ground yourself and cleanse your chakras (but in different ways,) then on one side you're led to the sanctuary of your choice. The other side then gets you in touch with your Higher Self.

ASCENSION - Experience yourself rising up into the higher dimensions, and becoming one with the universe as your receive your guidance in the higher realms.

GOING INTO MT. SHASTA - Mt. Shasta is a retreat for Ascended Masters. Experience the powerful energies of the mountain as you see and feel the presence of Masters and feel yourself in the mountains healing pool.

All Tapes are $12.00 each. Price includes Shipping & Handling.

Vanishing Veil

USA ORDER FORM

_____ MEDITATION AT THE BEACH   _____ ASCENSION
_____ RELATIONSHIPS   _____ THUNDERSTORM MEDITATION
_____ FORGIVE AND RELEASE   _____ GOING INTO MT. SHASTA
_____ ASTRAL FLIGHT
_____ GETTING IN TOUCH WITH YOUR HIGHER SELF
     & CREATING YOUR OWN SANCTUARY

All Tapes are **$12.00** each. Price includes Shipping & Handling all tapes shipped to CA add 7% tax

_____ **VANISHING VEIL $14.95** (S&H $3.50 ground $0.75 each additial book or Priority 2-3 day service $5.50 $1.00 each additional book) all books shipped to CA add 7% tax

Name:_____
Address:_____
City:_____State:____ Zip:_____
Phone: _____
Card number _____
Exp.Date ___/___ Name on Card: _____

VISA and MASTERCARD   OR
MAKE CHECKS PAYABLE TO:

Marge Cuddeback   6981 Elwood Rd. San Jose, CA 95120
   (408) 997-1869   margec@earthlink.net

You may copy this form.

204

Seminars

If you are interested in any seminar or would like to organize a group in your area, I can travel to your city. Please contact me for further information (408) 997-1869   margec@earthlink.net

BEGINNING YOUR INTUITIVE SEARCH

Don't put off developing your sixth sense any longer. Realize that we truly do create and control our own destiny. There's been a tremendous shift of consciousness in the universe. **Be a part of it!**

I call my first seminar, "Beginning your Intuitive Search". It's meant for anyone interested in learning a basic understanding of psychic phenomena. In this seminar we'll discuss and experience:

1. Meditation
2. Auras
3. Psychometry
4. Learning to trust your inner voice
5. Many ways of making contact with loved ones who have crossed over
6. Radionics (using a pendulum to get your answers)
7. How to create and control your own destiny (Learn the power of your mind through mental telepathy.)
8. Introduction to various forms of healing
9. Visualization (how to manifest people and objects into your life)
10. Automatic writing (receiving guidance from your Higher Self, guides, or loved ones on the other side)
11. Reincarnation, and how our past lives effect where we are today
12. Astral Projection

Vanishing Veil

Expanding Your Spiritual Growth

In this seminar I cover:
1. Deeper forms of meditation.
2. Visualization (learn to manifest people, objects and/or abundance into your life).
3. Chakras (the energy centers of your body).
4. Grounding yourself.
5. Creating your own sanctuary.
6. Getting in touch with your Higher Self.
7. Meeting up with your spiritual guide.
8. Mini readings (learn to trust your intuition).
9. I'll take you on a group regression into a past life.
10. Affirmations (a positive way to either change something or bring something or someone into your life).

Healing Seminar

The main focus of this seminar will be to learn how to take yourself and others to the source of their illness. You will also learn how to send loving, healing energies to yourself and others.

We all have the power within us to cure ourselves and others. Learn to heal yourself **BEFORE** an illness manifests itself. You need to go to the source of your illness. Unless you learn how to release those buried resentments, angers, heartaches and negative thoughts, those negatives will manifest themselves in the physical form of an illness. We need to heal not only our physical body, but also our mental, emotional and spiritual self.

SEMINARS

REGRESSION SEMINAR

In this seminar, I'll take you on approximately five different types of regressions. You'll have the chance to go back to the cause of something happening in your life now that you want to explore. If you are having career or relationship problems, that's a very good clue as to what your karmic lessons in this life are all about. Hopefully through wisdom and self-forgiveness while in a regression, you can start to move past your problems. Through this seminar you can discover your karmic ties with loved ones, and find out how you were related to them in a past life.

If you have headaches in this life, you may find out you were shot in the head or clubbed to death in a previous lifetime.

If you have insomnia problems, you may find out that you were molested or murdered in your sleep, and you carried that fear over from a past life. When you find out the cause, it's very often the end of your problem. Again, 'cause and effect'.

ASCENSION SEMINAR

We are in an exciting time frame, when the earth and most of the people on the earth will experience going from the third to the fifth dimension before the year 2012. In the fifth dimension, we can manifest people and things into our lives by simply thinking of them. We will communicate through telepathy. We will be able to physically transport ourselves through mental thought. It's the first dimension of heaven. You will be in your full consciousness.

In this seminar, we will discuss and experience:
1. Various Ascension techniques
2. Forgive and release techniques
3. Rejuvenation - DNA shift
4. Relationships
5. Ascension practices
6. Light body activation
7. The earth's future

Vanishing Veil

Awakening your Light Body Course

It's time to take the next gigantic step of your spiritual growth. Explore awakening your light body. This is a powerful year of spiritual transformation as new higher energies of light come to the earth plane. It is time to make a major shift in your consciousness, connect more strongly with your soul's light, and take the next steps toward manifesting your higher path. This course will help shift your vibratory note to a higher level.

Your light body is the spiritual shimmer that is the next evolutionary step for humanity. Your light body is a new energy body; a part of your aura that was not possible to awaken before the new, higher energies came to the earth plane. It is your aura as it exists in the higher dimensions of your soul. You will increase your ability to transform the energy around you into light, to become a clearer transmitter of light, and to experience the never-ending unfolding of these energies of light. You will find that the gridwork of light is available to each of you as a source of soul nourishment, stability, strength, energy and light.